Campden & Chorleywood Food
Research Association Group

D1740484

Key Topics in Food
Science and Technology – No. 7

# Food packaging:
# an introduction

## Tim Hutton

Campden & Chorleywood Food Research Association Group comprises
Campden & Chorleywood Food Research Association
and its subsidiary companies
CCFRA Technology Ltd     CCFRA Group Services Ltd     Campden & Chorleywood Magyarország

Campden & Chorleywood Food
Research Association Group

Chipping Campden, Gloucestershire, GL55 6LD  UK
Tel: +44 (0) 1386 842000   Fax: +44 (0) 1386 842100
www.campden.co.uk

Information emanating from this company is given after the exercise of all reasonable care
and skill in its compilation, preparation and issue, but is provided without liability in its
application and use.

The information contained in this publication must not be reproduced without permission
from the CCFRA Publications Manager.

Legislation changes frequently.  It is essential to confirm that legislation cited in this
publication and current at the time of printing is still in force before acting upon it.  Any
mention of specific products, companies or trademarks is for illustrative purposes only and
does not imply endorsement by CCFRA.

© CCFRA 2003
ISBN: 0 905942 61 2
*A catalogue record for this book is available from the British Library.*

# SERIES PREFACE

Food and food production have never had a higher profile, with food-related issues featuring in newspapers or on TV and radio almost every day. At the same time, educational opportunities related to food have never been greater. Food technology is taught in schools, as a subject in its own right, and there is a variety of food-related courses in colleges and universities - from food science and technology through nutrition and dietetics to catering and hospitality management.

Despite this attention, there is widespread misunderstanding of food - about what it is, about where it comes from, about how it is produced, and about its role in our lives. One reason for this, perhaps, is that the consumer has become distanced from the food production system as it has become much more sophisticated in response to the developing market for choice and convenience. Whilst other initiatives are addressing the issue of consumer awareness, feedback from the food industry itself and from the educational sector has highlighted the need for short focused overviews of specific aspects of food science and technology with an emphasis on industrial relevance.

The *Key Topics in Food Science and Technology* series of short books therefore sets out to describe some fundamentals of food and food production and, in addressing a specific topic, each issue emphasises the principles and illustrates their application through industrial examples. Although aimed primarily at food industry recruits and trainees, the series will also be of interest to those interested in a career in the food industry, food science and technology students, food technology teachers, trainee enforcement officers and, established personnel within industry seeking a broad overview of particular topics.

Leighton Jones
Series Editor

# PREFACE TO THIS VOLUME

Most foods in retail outlets are sold pre-packed. Usually, the packaging is more than a handy container: it is an essential barrier to harmful micro-organisms or chemicals, provides protection from physical damage, carries consumer information, and is an important marketing tool. In short, it is an integral part of the product. Often, in fact, food product development is stimulated by innovations in packaging. At the same time, environmental pressures - such as minimisation of waste and energy usage - are providing the impetus for new approaches to product packaging.

This book sets out to provide an introduction to food packaging within the context of the modern food industry. It starts by establishing the perspective that the packaging is an integral part of the product, and then describes each of the main types of packaging in turn - metal, glass, paper and board, and plastics - outlining the nature of the materials concerned and the benefits and limitations of each. It looks at the main functions of packaging, covering its roles in food safety, physical protection, marketing and conveying information. This leads into an example-based discussion of the importance of compatibility between the food, the process and the package, and how this has culminated with developments such as modified atmosphere packaging, active packaging and intelligent packaging. The growing role of environmental issues in shaping decisions on packaging is also considered.

The intention is to describe the main principles underlying the use of, innovations in, and pressures on food packaging, and to illustrate these with everyday industrially relevant examples. This, together with the list of carefully chosen references, should provide a useful starting point to anyone who wishes to understand more about food packaging or to pursue the subject in greater depth.

Tim Hutton

## ACKNOWLEDGEMENTS

My thanks go to all staff, past and present, at CCFRA whose work I consulted in producing this overview, and particularly those whose expertise I called upon in reviewing the text: Professor Colin Dennis, Alan Campbell, Greg Hooper and Leighton Jones.

## NOTE

All definitions, legislation, codes of practice and guidelines mentioned in this publication are included for the purposes of illustration only and relate to UK practice unless otherwise stated.

# CONTENTS

# 1. INTRODUCTION

Food packaging plays a vital role in the delivery of the food commodity from the manufacturer to the customer or consumer. In general terms, it must prevent the contents from escaping, and prevent external objects getting in. It must also be compatible with the required transport and storage conditions (e.g. temperature), and thus keep the food in the desired physical, chemical and microbiological state. As such it is no different to any other packaged commodity, although there are several factors that are particularly important in food packaging - the prevention of contamination (microbial, physical or chemical) being one such factor. The many requirements for packaging (such as 'tamper-evident' seals) can sometimes result in what may be seen by some as unnecessary extra packaging. It is unusual for there to be no good reason for the apparent over-packaging of a food product. Packaging is expensive and all companies producing packaged foods will look at ways of reducing packaging costs, if it can be achieved without any loss in product quality or safety.

The type of packaging used will depend on the nature of the food and the processing and storage conditions to which it is going to be subjected. Also of importance are the types of functions that the packaging will have to fulfil; for example, does it need to be permeable to allow gas exchange, as in modified atmosphere packaging of fresh fruit or vegetables, or does it have a role to play in the cooking of the product, as in a microwaveable pack? In some cases, the shape of the packaging (and possibly therefore the type used), will be constrained by the food in question, or vice versa: rectangular sliced bread for sandwiches cut on the diagonal needs right-angled triangular sandwich boxes. However, within these broad constraints, there are many alternatives for what packaging material can be used, as exemplified in Table 1 for chilled food.

**Table 1 -** Types of packaging used in chilled foods (Day, 2000a)

| | |
|---|---|
| Aluminium foil | Plastics, e.g.: |
| Cardboard | polypropylene |
| Regenerated cellulose | polystyrene |
| Paper | polyvinyl chloride |
| Glass | polyethylene - high or low density |
| Natural casings | polyethylene terephthalate |
| Paper | cellulose acetate |
| Metallised board | ethylene-vinyl acetate |
| Metallised film | polyvinylidene chloride |
| Steel | nylon |

The over-riding importance of food packaging is to enable the manufacturer to effect delivery of the food to the consumer in the best possible condition. This usually means as near as possible to its condition when it left the manufacturer, although in some cases, it may be desirable for a controlled change to occur during the time it is in transit (e.g. ripening of fruit and vegetables, and maturation of cheeses). Thus, packaging must be designed to prevent unwanted ingress of pathogens or spoilage micro-organisms, toxic or tainting chemicals, or physical contaminants (insects, metal, glass, stones etc.). It must also not adversely pass its own constituents (chemical or physical) to the product, and should not support microbial growth that would adversely affect the product.

As well as preventing contamination, packaging must also keep the food in a desirable condition, by preventing physical damage to the food (e.g. maintaining the structure of jam tarts), and by preventing or retarding undesirable intrinsic chemical or microbial changes. The packaging may even go further, and be designed to promote desirable chemical and microbiological changes (so-called 'active' packaging).

Finally, packaging must convey to the consumer the nature of the contents. There are legal requirements for naming the products and its ingredients, and indicating the number, weight or volume of product inside the package. There are also strong marketing drivers for making the packaging look appealing. These are very much consumer-driven: when product developers are thinking of new ideas, the question of whether to use glass, metal or plastic, for example, for the product must take into consideration consumer preferences as well as a knowledge of what effect the individual packaging types might have on the product. Also, if the consumer had no preference for pictorial designs on packaging, there would be no gain in the manufacturer spending time, effort and money coming up with appealing designs.

With most food types there is usually more than one form of packaging that will provide broadly the same characteristics. Often the same product will be available in different forms of packaging from different manufacturers, or the same manufacturer may offer largely the same product in different ways - either for different occasions (e.g. single and multi-serve sizes) or to create a different image. Sometimes, the product's demands are not very restrictive - olive oil, for example, is packaged in glass and plastic bottles, and also in metal drums. The possibilities and combinations are almost endless, and in most cases it is not possible to define the ideal package for any particular food. There are always trade-offs to be considered. The development of plastics technology means that the physical characteristics of plastics packages can be engineered very precisely, resulting in containers that may be improved in functionality compared with, say, a paper or board version. However, paper and board are both biodegradable and derived from renewable resources, immediately creating a dilemma as to which is the better option.

The purpose of this Key Topic is to look at the characteristics of each of the main packaging materials, primarily from a scientific/technological standpoint. It will also look at the circumstances in which they are regularly used, discussing the functions that they can perform in relation to the needs of the product, although, in doing this, it is not possible to look at every food/packaging combination.

# 2. MAJOR PACKAGING TYPES

Various materials are used to package food - mostly metal, glass, plastic and paper/board in various combinations. The production of these materials, by the raw material manufacturer, and their conversion into the finished packaging form, are highly developed scientific and technical disciplines. To ensure that they are fit for their intended purpose requires detailed and accurate specifications and knowledge of the needs of the particular food and of the properties of the packaging and the material from which it is made. The detailed monitoring of formulation and production of packaging is outside the scope of this book, but the reader is referred to the Technical Standard produced by the British Retail Consortium and Institute of Packaging as an example (BRC, 2002). This section looks at looks at packaging from the viewpoint of the materials; it necessarily strays into considerations of package-product interactions from time to time, although aspects of this are covered in more detail in chapter 4.

## 2.1 Metal

The rigidity and non-breakable nature of metal makes it an ideal candidate as a food packaging material. These physical attributes lend themselves to situations such as biscuit barrels or large confectionery containers, where the ability to mould and engrave designs onto the outside of the package make metal particularly useful for creating attractive and appealing designs for relatively high-value and small-volume (in terms of numbers of items) products. Metal is also used in conjunction with other materials to form laminate composites; for example, a layer of aluminium is incorporated with layers of paperboard and plastic in the formation of long-life soft drinks cartons.

Metals are very good light and oxygen barriers (although the barrier to oxygen will rely on an hermetic seal being formed in the package), and they can stand extremes of temperature, from sterilisation temperatures (typically 121°C) to below 0°C.

However, they cannot be used for products that are designed for microwave heating, unless they have been coated, typically with plastic. (See chapter 4 for a summary of the problems of metal usage in microwaves). Metal is also potentially subject to corrosion by the food it contains, primarily from wet (especially highly acidic) food and in the presence of oxygen. Therefore, it is most suitable for dry, ambient-stable products, or those that are hermetically sealed with the exclusion of oxygen. The problem of corrosion can be mitigated by the use of coatings, such as lacquers on cans.

The two metals commonly used as the major component of food packaging are steel and aluminium. Relatively thick steel-based materials are used in canned foods, while thinner aluminium cans are used for soft drinks, and very thin films are used as foil laminates (e.g. as peel-off lids).

**Metal cans**

Metal containers can come in many different forms, but it is for shelf-stable, heat-processed food, in the form of the can, that metal has had its greatest success as a

## Box 1 - Metal types for different purposes

**Tinplate steel** - steel coated with tin - the most widely used metal in both two-piece (including drawn wall-ironed [DWI]) and three-piece food cans. Of varying thickness (generally 0.17 to 0.25mm), depending on end use, and container size and method of manufacture. Tin coating weight also varies, as does the composition of the low-carbon steel.

**Tin-free steel** - electro-chromium coated steel. A mild steel with a chromium/chromium oxide surface treatment. Used in two-piece draw-redraw (DRD) containers (i.e. cans in which the base and body are formed in two stages from an intact, flat piece of steel), and for non-easy open ends (i.e. non-ring pull ends)

**Aluminium** - foils used extensively for trays (e.g. for reheatable ready meals) and film lids (often in conjunction with other forms of packaging). Also for easy-open ends and for two-piece DWI beverage cans and closures and some food cans food packaging material. Many processes can be applied to metal containers, but this section will concentrate on those that are particularly relevant to the requirements of the sterilised food can. The metal can also provides an excellent snapshot of the constraints arising from packaging/food interactions.

From its initial development in the early 1800's to its worldwide development and distribution through the ensuing 100 years, the heat-processed metal can has probably had the biggest single impact in the history of the modern food processing industry. It was the first major example of a convenience food, enabling fruit, vegetable and meat products to be made available to the consumer throughout the year in a form not too dissimilar to that previously available (e.g. fresh, cooked fruit and vegetables and cooked meats from specialist shops), and for these products to be stored at ambient temperatures by the consumer for years rather than days.

The development of heat processing as a method of long-term preservation of food occurred hand-in-hand with the development of the metal food can as a packaging form. The preservation method, in most cases, involves the elimination of all intrinsic microbial and enzymic activity (in some special circumstances, viable micro-organisms may remain in the can, but will be inactive because of the nature of the food, such as its sugar or salt content or acidity). This is called commercial sterilisation. The design of the can enables all extrinsic spoilage agents to be kept out of the food. The body of the can is filled with the foodstuff, the lid is put on and sealed and the can is sterilised. The relatively small amount of headspace, and the partial vacuum that can be created during the process, mean that only a small amount of oxygen remains in the can, which results in a much reduced rate of chemical changes such as oxidative rancidity.

The standard process to achieve commercial sterilisation is equivalent to 3 minutes at 121°C in the slowest heating point of the food (higher temperature/shorter time or lower temperature/longer time combinations can be used to achieve the same degree of processing). The actual process applied varies from product to product, but the important thing to note from the packaging point of view is that it will have to withstand a significant period of time at temperatures well above the boiling point of water. In fact, superheated steam is typical of the type of medium used to heat the cans. This level of heat processing is required in metal cans because of the anaerobic environment created in the can, which could allow the growth of spores of *Clostridium botulinum*, which produce a highly potent neurotoxin. The spores themselves are very heat resistant and the standard process is designed to reduce the likelihood of their survival to 1 in one million million.

Nicholas Appert was the first to discover that food could be preserved by heating it in a sealed container; he actually used corked, wide-mouth glass bottles for his work (the term canning actually refers to the heating in a sealed container, not to the metallic nature of the container). In 1810, Peter Durand was granted a patent for the technique using sealed metal containers (Lopez, 1987). The first metal cans for food were cylinders of steel formed by soldering a sheet of metal with lead; bases and lids were similarly soldered on to form an hermetic seal. Nowadays, soldering has largely been replaced in the food industry throughout the world - principally because of concerns about lead intake via foods: today, side seams are generally welded, and bases and lids are mechanically seamed (described below).

Tinplate is the principal material used for metal boxes and food cans, although aluminium is also widely used, principally for drinks cans, and tin-free steel is also used (the latter is steel coated with a layer of chromium and chromium oxide instead of tin). Tinplate is mild steel (i.e. a low-carbon steel) coated on both sides with tin (hence the name tin cans), generally using electrolytic techniques (Turner, 1998).

Nowadays, for both tinplate and tin-free steel, the base steel is usually cast in a continuous process, which allows all of the impurities to float on top of the molten metal, thus allowing a much cleaner steel to be produced (Page, 2001). The resulting steel slab is hot rolled into a coil of about 2mm thickness, which can be subsequently cold-rolled to the required final thickness. After each cold rolling, the metal has to be annealed (i.e. heated to high temperature), to relieve some of the stresses induced by cold rolling. This is normally done in a continuous process: the coil of steel is unwound and passed through an oven at high speed, and subsequently cooled and rewound. Various techniques are used to harden the metal - improvements in these in the last 30-40 years have enabled a significant reduction in the thickness of food cans to be made without any loss in strength or structural integrity (Paine and Paine, 1983). Coils of this metal, or pre-cut sheets are then formed into cans in a number of ways - the main steps used and alternatives available are as follows.

Cans can either be either two-piece or three-piece. In two piece cans, the body wall and one integral end are formed from one piece of flat metal without any seams by using various mechanical pressing techniques. This is called drawing. In redrawing, the cylinder is further pressed to form a longer cylinder of smaller cross-section (DRD). Drawn cans can also be 'ironed' (DWI), a process in which the thickness of the metal is reduced in one or more stages by up to 70%; this allows the height of the can to be increased without changing its diameter. Tinplate and aluminium cans are commonly produced in this way.

In three-piece cans, the sheet metal is formed into a cylinder, and the edges are joined, usually by welding, where an electric current is passed across the two layers of metal to be joined, thus heating them so that they can be mechanically squeezed together. Most 3-piece cans are made of tinplate; tin-free steel is difficult to weld and is usually formed by the DRD method.

After the basic cylinder has been formed, further processes may be required to make the container fit for its intended use. In all cases, a flange or lip needs to be made at the top of the can, so that the lid can be fitted (in three-piece cans, a flange for the base also needs to be formed). This flange may be curled, to make the edge safer and improve the appearance of the finished can.

One or both ends of the cylinder may also be reduced in diameter, while leaving the main body diameter unchanged (a process known as inward necking). These and other treatments such as embossing, base reforming and washing of the cans are described in some detail by Page (2001).

The final major stage in producing a can is the mechanical seaming of ends onto can bodies. The seams have to be able to withstand changes in temperature and pressure encountered during processing, and maintain their integrity to prevent the micro-leaking of bacteria after processing. In some situations, such as with carbonated drinks and aerosols, high internal pressures may occur, and the seams must prevent leakage of product. The mechanical seam is formed by bringing together the preformed seaming panel or curl of the lid with the flange of the can body, also incorporating a lining compound. The edges are turned down through 90°, and then the whole of the circumference of the rim is tightened to effect an hermetic seal.

# Typical cross-section of can wall/lid seam

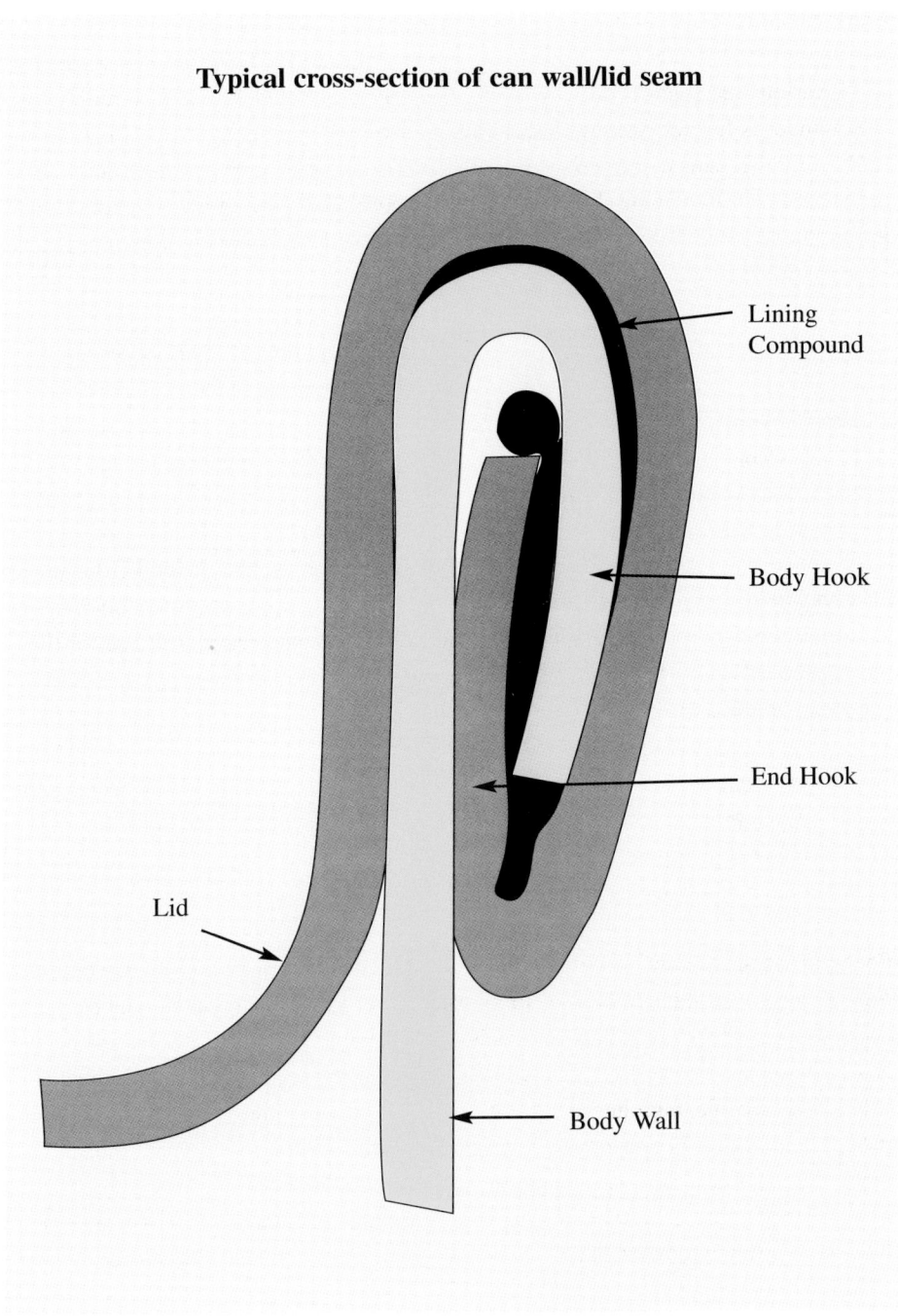

Lining Compound

Body Hook

End Hook

Lid

Body Wall

---

**Box 2 - Preventing can defects**

As cans are usually designed for prolonged storage of foods, it is important to prevent can damage, which would compromise the safety of the food. There are many stages during the lifetime of the can that could potentially give rise to a problem. (See Thorpe (1994) for further details.) These include:

- manufacturing operations: faults to either the can or the lid
- receipt, storage and conveying of the empty can to the filling area: corrosion from rain, and physical damage because of poor loading, palleting or driving of fork-lift truck
- can filling operations: physical damage to the can or incorrect alignment or sealing of the lid
- can transport prior to retorting (sterilisation): physical damage through poor handling during transport or loading into the retort
- processing operations: corrosion because of poor quality sterilising water or excess oxygen in the retort, or too much chlorine in the cooling water
- post-processing operations: corrosion and physical damage during cooling and transport of the final cooled product respectively

---

A great variety of food types can be packed in metal cans; however, many of these foods could potentially interact chemically with the metal of the can. For this reason, various lacquer coatings can be applied to the inside of the can to prevent certain reactions and promote others. The coatings are made up of complex blends of resins in a solvent mixture with specific additives for different functions. For example:

- aluminium flakes may be incorporated into the lacquer to mask sulphur staining (the formation of black metal sulphides) in canned meat and fish products
- lubricants may be incorporated to help the consumer remove the food from the can
- pigments may be added for enhanced appearance - titanium dioxide is used to give a white colour to the lacquer

## Box 3 - Metal lacquers in the food industry

Oleo-resinous lacquers have the longest history of use in the food industry. They are made by fusing natural gums and resins and blending them with drying oils such as linseed oil and wood (tung) oil. Although their use in the UK has largely been superseded by epoxyphenolics, they may still be found in imported products.

Vinyl lacquers are made by dissolving co-polymers of vinyl chloride and vinyl acetate in suitable solvents. They may be blended with other resins and pigmented if required. They offer good flexibility and adhesion, particularly on aluminium (although their use in beverage cans has been superseded by water-based lacquers). They remain the lacquer of choice for both the interior and exterior of dry food containers.

Phenolic lacquers are made by the reaction of phenol with formaldehyde. Hard films with low flexibility result, but they are highly resistant to sulphur staining (the formation of metal sulphides - usually black in colour - on the inside of the can), and so are very suitable for high-sulphur foods, such as meat, peas and beans. They develop a characteristic gold colour on storage.

Epoxy resins are based on epichlorhydrin and diphenylol-propane. Their combined properties of flexibility, chemical resistance and good adhesion to the metal base mean that they are suitable for use with a wide variety of foods, such as meat, fish, fruit and vegetables.

The use of polyester-phenolic lacquers has grown in recent years. They have similar properties to epoxy lacquers, and are usually gold in colour. Aluminium pigment or zinc oxide/carbonate can be incorporated to reduce sulphur staining.

Water-based lacquers are principally used on two-piece beer and soft drink cans. They are usually based on a high-molecular-weight epoxy resin and a high acid acrylic resin dispersed in water.

## Box 4 - Tin in food

Although there is no evidence that excess tin intake has any long-term health effects, some studies have shown that intake of high concentrations (above about 250ppm) may cause short-term gastrointestinal problems. In view of this, in the UK there is a general upper limit of 200ppm (mg/kg) for tin in all foods, and it is likely that the European Union will adopt this level across all member states in the near future. For most foods, the general maximum limit for tin is of no significance, but for foods packed in cans with some unlacquered tinplate, the upper limit can occasionally be exceeded. Tin dissolution in unlacquered tinplate cans is essential in that it confers electrochemical protection to the iron, which makes up the structural component of the can and so maintains the can's integrity. Without it, the can would quickly become corroded by the contents; this could cause serious discoloration and off-flavours in the product and swelling of the can. Tin is also involved in maintaining product quality (it helps prevent undesirable colour changes amongst other things, by mopping up any residual oxygen left in the headspace), so there is an advantage in some products of having some exposed (i.e. unlacquered) tinplate. As tin dissolution tends to be accelerated by oxygen, for products where exposed tin is considered to be beneficial, the base, lid and ends of the can may be lacquered, with the rest being unlacquered.

Tin pick-up is normally relatively slow and does not give rise to excessive levels in the product within its shelf-life. However, certain natural variations within the product can cause problems. These include its acidity, the presence of certain organic acids and pigments, and elevated levels of nitrates and sulphides. In addition, the amount of air in the headspace and the thickness of the tin coating also have an effect. Although the thickness of the tin coating will ultimately limit the maximum possible level of tin in the product, the rate of pick-up may be increased when thinner coatings are used.

In a survey by the then Ministry of Agriculture, Fisheries and Food, elevated levels of tin (although normally still within the legal maximum) were found in canned asparagus, tomatoes, apricots, grapefruit and gooseberries. Subsequently, a report from Finland suggested that high levels could also be found in canned grapefruit. Studies at CCFRA confirmed that high levels could be found canned tomato, pineapple and other products, but that excessive levels were very unusual and that there was no specific cause to which these levels could be attributed.

continued...

There have been several attempts to mimic beneficial effects of tinplate, e.g. by introducing tin into the lacquer coatings or by adding permitted tin salts to the products, but none has been as effective as having the tin dissolve from the tinplate itself. Because of concerns over tin levels in some of these foods, the use of fully lacquered cans has become more widespread. For some products for which tin dissolution is particularly important, it is claimed that this has resulted in some loss of product quality.

**Further reading:**

Edwards, M. (1999) Investigation of the sources of tin in canned foods. CCFRA R&D Report 79

Edwards, M. (1999) A survey of tin content of canned pineapple products. CCFRA R&D Report 93

Edwards, M. (1999) A survey of tin content of canned tomatoes and tomato based products. CCFRA R&D Report 96

Ministry of Agriculture, Fisheries and Food (1997). Survey of lead and tin in canned fruit and vegetables. MAFF Food Surveillance Information Sheet No. 122

Tin in Food Regulations 1992 Statutory Instrument No. 496 (UK)

There are two good examples of where processing innovations are closely linked with the nature and form of the packaging: ring-pull ends, which are essential for packaging ready-to-serve drinks in cans, and the widget, designed for use in beer cans - although technology has subsequently been developed to allow this to be replicated in bottles (see boxes 5 and 6).

## Box 5 - Easy-open or ring-pull ends

Easy-open ends for foods and drinks are based on the same primary aim: to partially cut through (or score) the metal in the lid, so that with the aid of an attached key or tab, the scored metal can be torn off manually by the consumer. With food cans, the aim is to pull off the entire end portion of the lid (leaving just the original edge seal attached to the body of the can). With drinks the aim is to remove just a small section of the lid.

The first easy-open ends were manufactured for drinks cans and were made of aluminium. Before this development, the lids of containers had to be punctured twice with a sharp metal tool, with one hole to pour out the liquid and the other to allow air into the container to facilitate pouring. This requirement severely limited the development of drinks in cans. Initially the ring-pull was attached to the tear-off tab, and the whole section was removed from the can and often discarded. The removed metal can be quite sharp, and this poses both safety and environmental concerns. Most forms of ring-pull end result in the scored tab remaining attached to the can (usually dipping approximately vertically into the drink).

The degree of scoring on the lid for both foods and drinks has to be very precise, so that the consumer can relatively easily pull off the lid, but that the hermetic seal is not compromised (i.e. the lid is not punctured during the scoring process and the scored section does not come off during transport and handling operations). The metal thickness in can ends is about 0.22mm (Page, 2001). In aluminium ends, the scoring leaves a thickness of about 50% in the scored section. In food cans with steel ends, the thickness in the scored section is about 25% of the thickness of the lid. From a ring-pull perspective, aluminium ends are preferred, because it takes less force to open them, and a greater metal residual thickness can be left in the scored section. However, most food cans are made of steel, and steel easy-open ends are generally used to avoid the problem of corrosion that can occur at the seam when two dissimilar metals are joined (Page, 2001).

## Box 6 - The widget

The widget is a good example of the needs of the product influencing packaging design, and spawning a new packaging development. Some bottled beers have existed for many years and have evolved or been developed into popular products with distinct characteristics of their own (e.g. Worthington 'White Shield' which is fermented in the bottle). However, many products are intended to be canned or bottled varieties of the 'draught' equivalent. One of the major problems with this was the inability of the canned or bottled product to produce a 'head', similar to that of the draught beer, when poured out. Although the beverage in the bottle is carbonated, the release of gas on opening does not mimic the effects of pulling draught beer. The problem is compounded in stouts like Guinness, which are less fizzy than lagers and some bitters (i.e. they contain less dissolved carbon dioxide, and so less is released on opening the can or bottle).

The Guinness company developed and introduced an insert (which they called a widget) in the mid to late 1980s to help achieve a 'smoother' Guinness pint. Nearly 30 alternative designs were considered before a nitrogen filler design was adopted - it was appreciated early on that removal of oxygen from the device was a key factor (Browne, 1996). Many other brewers have subsequently incorporated widget designs into their own beers.

There are now many different variations on widget design. The widget originally developed by Guinness and described in US Patent 4832968 is a small plastic hollow pod with a minute hole in it. It is placed inside the can during the first stage of the packaging process. When the can has been filled with drink, sealed and chilled, the drink inside the can becomes naturally pressurized (in some beverages, a small amount of liquid nitrogen can be included before closure to increase pressurization). This pressure forces around 1% of the drink inside the widget, in turn pressurising the gas (nitrogen) within. The widget has a small chamber inside that is specifically designed to hold a small amount of drink, which flows in through a very small opening in the underside of the widget.

When the can is opened, the contents reach normal atmospheric pressure. The drink that is held inside the chamber of the widget is forced out through the small opening in the widget as the pressure inside and outside the can equalize. The effect is to release millions of tiny bubbles of carbon dioxide from the drink, which rise to the surface and form the familiar, creamy head of a draught beer or stout. The key difference between the widget system and straightforward opening of a can is the greater number and smaller size of the bubbles released.

Widgets have been designed which are either attached to the can, or float on the surface. Variations have also been developed for use in bottles (Anon, 1996c).

## 2.2 Glass

Glass is one of the oldest packaging materials used for food (glass containers date back to the 1st century BC), and is suitable for a range of products. It can be hot-filled (e.g. with jam or sauces), thermally processed (in a similar way to metal cans - indeed, the early work on heat processed containers was done using glass rather than metal cans), and stored chilled (e.g. milk). The relative ease of forming a screw thread in glass means that closures (lids) can be easily made resealable. Its chemical inertness means that any type of product can be packed in glass, and its clarity means that it may present the food to its best advantage. This versatility and good marketing characteristics have resulted in a significant resurgence in the use of glass packaging for certain types of products.

However, glass is not suitable for storing products in the frozen state, as it is likely to crack on freezing, as water, the main component of most food, expands as it freezes. Indeed, its susceptibility to breakage is the main drawback in its use. Broken glass is highly hazardous, both to the food processor and packager, and to the consumer (see box 7). The other significant drawback to using glass is its weight - in order to minimise the susceptibility to breakage, glass containers have to be relatively thick, which means that they are significantly heavier than their plastic or metal equivalent, despite its relatively low density ($2.5g/cm^3$ - similar to aluminium) (Bakker, 1986).

There are also potential problems with light-mediated deterioration of some food types; vitamin B3, for example, for which milk is a good source, is degraded by light, as are many natural plant pigments that may be present in the food. Some of these problems can be reduced by the use of coloured glass (e.g. white wine in green or brown bottles).

Although the raw materials for glass manufacture are relatively cheap, the production costs, especially in terms of energy usage, are quite high.

## Box 7 - Glass breakages

The susceptibility of glass to breakage is one of the main drawbacks to its use. In the home it can result in the scatter of large and small fragments of very sharp splinters; as most glass used in food packaging is clear, the smaller pieces are likely to be very difficult to see and a thorough clean-up of the area is necessary.

In a food processing environment, the situation could have serious consequences. Breakages could arise from mis-aligned filling or closure equipment, abrasion between containers on conveyor belts, or the containers simply falling off the processing line. In some instances, the breakages may be too slight to be immediately obvious, which is potentially a very dangerous situation, with the possibility of small fragments of glass getting into the food itself. It is essential that all food manufacturing operations that involve glass have a comprehensive glass breakage procedure, as well as controls to minimise the possibility of it happening. This has to take into account the fact that product may have been spilled, and so a general clean-up procedure may also be required. Rose and Gaze (1998) document a typical generic procedure. They suggest that as a matter of good manufacturing practice, the processing line should be inspected at 30-minute intervals to ensure that no broken glass is evident.

Typically, if a breakage is discovered, the following procedure is undertaken:

- Stop the processing line immediately
- Remove and discard all glass containers from the affected equipment
- Discard the established number of containers pre- and post-breakage point, together with any additional containers which are thought may have been contaminated with glass or damaged
- Collect all broken glass, paying particular attention to ledges, belts, and the underside of filling valves
- Ensure that the line and surrounding areas are clean and free from all glass fragments. Wash the area, if needed, with a low-pressure hose
- Remove and discard the first containers through the operation after the restart
- If the breakage does not appear to have been discovered immediately, all production since the last clear-line glass inspection must be held for inspection

Importantly, the production line can not be restarted until the cause of the breakage has been investigated. This can potentially result in significant financial loss.

*What is glass made of?*

The main constituent of practically all commercial glasses is sand. Sand by itself can be fused to produce glass, but it needs to be heated to about 1700°C to achieve this. Including sodium carbonate (soda ash) in about a 1:3 or 1:4 ratio reduces the temperature of fusion to about 800°C, yielding a mixture of silica and sodium oxide (carbon dioxide is released in the melting process), but this end-product is actually water soluble and is known as water glass. It is stabilized by the addition of calcium oxide and magnesium oxide, again in the form of the respective carbonates. Aluminium oxide is also added. This final basic product is known as soda-lime glass and is the material out of which window panes, drinking glasses and food packaging material are made. The other two main groups of commercially produced glass are: lead glass, in which lead oxide and potassium oxide replace calcium oxide and sodium oxide, respectively; and borosilicate glass, which contains 7-13% boric oxide, but these are not used as food packaging (British Glass, 1992).

Unless the raw materials used in the manufacturing process are very pure the glass produced will be tinted, normally green due to low levels of iron oxide (as little as 0.1%). However, highly purified materials are expensive and so other materials are added to the mixture to counter the effects. Selenium (pink) and cobalt (blue) can be used to counter the effects of iron. Adding higher levels of the minor constituents and in different combinations can produce an almost limitless variety of different shades and colours of glass (see British Glass, 1992 for a table of the most commonly used elements), which is a feature of some food and drink product packaging. A pale green glass can be produced by iron oxide levels of 0.15%. Chromium is also used to produce green glass; cobalt oxide is used for blue glass; and mixtures of iron, sulphur and carbon are used to produce amber and brown glass.

Cooling the fused material down quickly prevents crystallization, resulting in transparent glass. Translucent or opalescent glass is produced by slowing down the rate of cooling to produce a pre-determined level of crystal formation.

## Box 8 - Use of recycled glass

Broken glass is known as cullet - it can come direct from the factory or from an external source such as recycling bottle banks. Provided that it is of the desired colour and correct chemical composition, there is no limit to how much cullet can be used in any particular batch. Green glass can contain up to 95% cullet, and on average about 30% of all glass packaging comes from recycled material. The ability to use this material is facilitated by standardization of container glass compositions across manufacturers, so that its original source is unimportant. However, different colours can not be mixed, and it is important that the cullet is free from impurities, especially metals and ceramics, which would otherwise affect the colour and other properties of the final product.

*How are glass containers made?*

Until the second half of the 19th Century, bottles and jars were made individually by mouth blowing and finishing the neck (for fixing the lid or closure) by manual manipulation with simple tools. The mouth of the bottle, being the last bit to be formed, was known as the 'finish'. When it was discovered that the finish could be made first, a semi-automatic mechanism was developed for container manufacture. The part that was still manual was the initial pouring of the glass into the initial mould and using hand shears to cut it off when it was judged that right amount had been poured in. Nowadays, for container production for the food industry, the whole process is fully automated (British Glass, 1992; 1996).

Raw materials are automatically mixed and heated to 1500°C in a furnace. Measured portions of the molten glass are then fed into a machine where they are automatically shaped in a two-stage process. For narrow-neck containers, the neck is formed and an initial 'blank' shape (known as a parison) is blown. This basic shape is then transferred to a second mould, where the final shape is blown. For wide-mouthed containers, a plunger presses out the initial blank shape, before it is blown in a second mould.

When initially blown, the glass is very hot (around 500°C). However, it has a low thermal conductivity, which means that surfaces will cool significantly more quickly than the centre. This would produce uncontrolled strain in the container and make it very susceptible to thermal shock and breakage during use. This can be avoided by slow cooling at a controlled rate (called annealing) which occurs by conveyance through an oven called a lehr. The containers enter the lehr at about 450°C and are initially heated to about 560°C. This allows the glass to begin to flow. The containers are then slowly cooled as they move through the lehr, to a point where no further strain can be induced in them, after which they are air-cooled with a fan down to room temperature.

The weight of glass is a significant drawback in their use as food packaging, and so there has been a move to reducing the thickness of containers. This would have major repercussions regarding strength and resistance to breakage during processing and use, so toughening measures are required. These take the form of various glass surface treatments. Organic titanium or inorganic tin compounds can be sprayed onto the containers whilst they are still hot (i.e. before they are annealed). This produces a very thin layer of metal within the surface of the glass, and approximately doubles the strength of the container. In addition, an organic compound such as oleic acid can be applied as the container exits the lehr (at about 150°C). This increases the lubricity of the containers and enables them to move efficiently through high-speed filling lines. Alternatively, an aqueous suspension of low-molecular-weight ethylene polymer or copolymer can be applied.

*Glass packaging design*

Glass containers can be designed in a wide variety of shapes and sizes corresponding to both functional and marketing requirements. Despite the range of shape possibilities, the design must work within constraints for strength and safety. Carbonated beverages, for example, will always have circular or nearly circular cross sections, to maximise resistance to internal pressure. There will also be due notice taken of the resulting centre of gravity and size of the base, to ensure good stability: for this reason, the base will always be slightly concave. The type of glass used not only has to be compatible with the food it will contain, but also with the closure to be used; much care is taken to ensure that the combination of the three elements does not result in an unsafe end-product.

Strength can be enhanced by avoiding high shoulders, square body sections and single container-to-container contact points. Special attention is also given to the sidewall contact areas. Generous contact areas reduce impact damage and label protection panels remove the risk of label scuffing.

Modern three-dimensional computer-aided design systems are now commonly used in glassworks design centres. These are particularly valuable in ensuring coherent and reproducible geometry where complex and non-rounded shapes are involved. When linked to computer-aided mould manufacture, the same 3D geometry is used to construct the mould cavities and the need for patterns, templates and models is completely eliminated (Rose and Gaze, 1998).

## Box 9 - Closures for glass and plastic containers

Closure materials used for glass or plastic jars and bottles have to be compatible with both the container itself and the food with which it will come into contact. Closure design needs to take into account the food packaging operation - the closure must be easily handled on the filling line. In high-speed production lines the whole application and sealing/closing operation must be accomplished in a fraction of a second. The end product must both contain and protect the product. Whatever type of packaging material has been used to contain the product, the seal with the closure is the most likely place for the properties of the packaging to be negated. An incorrectly applied seal can mean the loss of gases, moisture or aroma volatiles from the product, or the entry of microbial or chemical contaminants.

Closures can be made of metal or plastic and can be either screw-on/screw-off or some sort of prise-off mechanism, which may or may not be resealable. The physical nature of the closure will depend on the needs of the food or drink, including whether or not the food has any significant shelf-life after opening. A product which is not suitable for storage after opening should not be packaged with a resealable closure mechanism, as it may lead the consumer to mis-use the product (Soroka *et al.*, 1996).

continued...

Plastic closures are widely used. Polypropylene is the most commonly used material, as it is economical, easy to mould and easily coloured. It is also ideal for creating 'hinged' closures, as it is tolerant to the type of continual flexing involved. Polyethylene is useful for closures where some deformation is required to open them (e.g. for snap-on tub lids). Metal closures are also still widely used, and can be made of either tinplate or aluminium.

Screw-cap closures are used for most bottle type applications, although metal press-on, prise-off caps are still used on beer bottles. These require a special tool to remove the cap, and in general, the need for such tools is seen as an undesirable obstacle for consumer acceptance of products. A variation of the screw-thread approach is the twist or lug closure, widely used in wide-necked jars. Although they are applied and removed with a twisting action similar to a screw thread, these usually require only a few degrees of rotation (usually less than 90°). This type of closure is unsuitable for plastic jars as the stresses in the thread area are too great. Plastic jars usually have a screw-cap lid.

In many situations, the closure needs an extra component to create a complete seal between the closure and the bottle or jar. The minor irregularities on bottle and jar closure areas means that special care has to be taken to ensure that an effective seal is created - in essence, a slightly flexible component that will mould to the top of the container. These components may be separate from the rest of the closure (early liners were thin cork sheets), or they may be incorporated into the closure itself. Many modern designs of plastic closures have internally moulded sealing structures.

Whatever the closure material and design, it must be able to rapidly apply it to the jar or bottle in a production line environment. This means proper alignment of the machinery, so that the closure area of the container is not deformed or damaged in any other way. With plastic containers, deformation may mean that the seal is not properly formed and that the safety of the product is compromised. With glass containers, deformation is unlikely, but minor mis-alignments of the machinery may result in breakage of the container, or worse, unseen splintering with splinters of glass entering the food.

**For more information on closure design, see:**

Soroka, W., Emblem, A. and Emblem, H. (1996). Fundamentals of Packaging Technology. Revised UK edition. Institute of Packaging

*Use of glass for specific foods and processes*

So why is glass used is certain situations, and why is it not suitable in others? In some cases, more suitable or cheaper alternatives have been found - sometimes the benefits of the alternatives are marginal, and the attractive appearance or traditional association of glass with a product means that glass continues to be used. In other cases, glass remains the most suitable material to use. Factors that might influence the food manufacturer's decision include cost, weight, marketing strategies, and the ease of changing processing equipment.

Glass jars have traditionally been used for products such as jams and marmalades. These can be 'hot-filled' into the container and a metal screw closure applied. The temperature of jam processing and filling is sufficient to kill all micro-organisms of concern that might be inherent in the product. Therefore, while the product remains unopened, microbial growth should not be a problem. Traditionally, the nature of the product (particularly its sugar content and acidity) has meant that it is also stable after opening. With lower sugar products, including reduced-sugar jams, refrigeration may be required after opening. The advantages of glass with this type of product include its inertness, the ease of opening and reclosing the container (to prevent foreign body entry over a long period of time), its rigidity (e.g. compared with a thin plastic) and its transparency.

Glass jars can also be used in the same way as metal cans, i.e. filled, closed and heat processed. Glass enables the product to be seen, and so is suitable for products that look attractive after processing (e.g. brightly coloured vegetables such as peppers). However, glass is much more expensive than metal, and so economically, it is only viable for more high-value products. Because of the attractive nature of the product packed in this way, a premium price can be levied.

Glass has been the traditional material for packaging liquid products like cordials, carbonated soft drinks, beers, milk, wine and oil. Wine in particular is extremely susceptible to taints and off-flavours, and a completely inert container is essential, as the product is likely to be stored for a considerable length of time. Coloured glass is used in some cases to prevent any light-mediated changes in composition. Glass is also associated with the high-value profile of wine. For beverages, especially carbonated beverages, the impermeability of glass to both oxygen and carbon dioxide is a major advantage. Its strength also means that it can withstand the high pressures which may build up in carbonated drinks.

Milk is unusual in that it is a high-volume, low-cost product short-shelf-life product packed in glass. The ability to reuse glass milk bottles simply by cleaning them has been the economic cornerstone of this product/package combination. As the economics of milk retailing have changed (i.e. supermarkets and other shops have become predominant over traditional doorstep deliveries), and suitable plastic materials have become available, the use of glass milk bottles has declined dramatically. Plastic is considerably cheaper and lighter, the latter meaning that milk can be sold in larger volumes than in glass bottles, which would be significantly heavier. Plastic bottles are not as breakable, are easy to reseal, and there are no problems with the transfer of taints from the plastic to the milk. Environmental issues regarding packaging waste may be alleviated by the increase in recycling of the packaging material (see chapter 6).

High-value oils, such as virgin olive oil, are generally packed in glass, whereas low-value products are usually packed in plastic. This is mainly a case of economics - the higher value placed on virgin and extra-virgin olive oil mean that it is economically viable to use glass. Concomitant with this, the use of glass gives the product a higher-value appearance, and allows the extra premium to be charged.

## Box 10 - Thermal shocking of glass

Although glass can withstand very high temperatures (up to 500°C), which means that glass bottles and jars are suitable for heat processing, it is susceptible to sudden temperature changes - thermal shock, e.g. if one surface is suddenly cooled while the other remains hot. The cooled surface will try and contract, but the hot surface will effectively prevent it from doing so, as the two surfaces are joined to each other. This creates a state of tension in the cooled surface and one of compression in the hot surface, which may lead to cracking of the glass. This degree of susceptibility depends on the chemical nature of the glass, and the thickness and shape of the container. In thinner containers, the change in temperature can be rapidly transmitted from one side to the other, making them less likely to break. Stresses are likely to greatest at the join between the base and the side wall of a container; avoiding abrupt joins, and using gentle curves at the joins mitigates against this (Paine and Paine, 1983).

Plastic or aluminium cans are used instead of glass nowadays for most soft drink products. However, many beers are still bottled - brown or green glass are traditionally used - as a result of the good marketing image and association with the product of this form of packaging, combined with its suitability for use (glass has excellent gas barrier properties).

## 2.3 Paper-based packaging

Plant-based materials are probably the oldest form of food packaging still in regular use in the industry. Although paper and paperboard are the main plant-based products used for food packaging, there are two other materials that need to be mentioned: wood and cork.

---

### Box 11 - Use of wood in food packaging

Although not widely used as a primary packaging material for food products, wood is still widely used in bulk packaging situations - for construction of boxes and pallets. Wood shares many of the advantages of other plant-based materials: it is derived from renewable resources, it is biodegradable, and it is a relatively cheap material. For its major applications in the food industry, these characteristics, its strength and resilience to physical abuse, and its lightness (wood is significantly lighter than metal) mean that it has been used in warehouse situations, where fork-lift trucks and other machinery are used. However, its overall strength does depend to a significant extent on the type of fastenings used to hold the individual pieces of wood together. Nails are the most commonly used fastenings in the construction of boxes, but staples, lag screws and bolts are also used. Steel nails and staples are regularly used for pallets.

Wood is not generally used as a primary food packaging material, although wooden tea chests were a major exception for many years. The risk of splinters in the food processing area and the difficulty in cleaning wood (which may lead to chemical or microbiological contamination problems) mean that its use is very limited.

## Box 12 - Use of cork as bottle stoppers

Cork has a long history of use in bottle closures. Originally developed in about the 5th Century BC, and becoming prominent in the era of the Roman Empire, it subsequently went into decline until after the Renaissance in the 16th Century, when its unique properties were fully employed. The primary role of the bottle stopper is to provide an air-tight and product-tight seal; cork is ideally suited to this. It is both compressible and elastic, highly impervious to air and water penetration and low in thermal conductivity. It provides a very efficient friction-hold seal, and was widely used until the advent of plastic closures and the standardised continuous-thread screw cap in the first third of the 20th Century.

Although its use has declined in most applications, it is only recently that it has begun to be replaced in its most traditional role, as a stopper for wine bottles. The problem of musty taint has been one of the driving forces behind this decline. A major pan-European project was undertaken in the mid-1990s to explore the causes of this taint and so attempt to reduce its occurrence. The taint is largely due to 2,4,6-trichloroanisole (TCA), produced by commonly occurring moulds before and during cork production and transportation. In addition, high levels of TCA can be related to the occurrence of a rare, but specific, cork defect: yellow taint. The geographical origin of the cork did not have any bearing on the occurrence of the taint, although cork taken from the foot of the tree sometimes had elevated levels of TCA. The contamination of the cork stopper, the bottle and the wine during transportation were shown to be potentially very significant issues. However, musty defects in wine are not always due to cork and TCA is a common cause of taint in other food and drink products.

### Further reading:

QUERCUS - Qualitative experiments to determine the components responsible and eliminate the causes of undesirable sensory characteristics in drinks stoppered with cork. European Communites Directorate-General XII. Contract No. AIR 1- CT92 - 0372.

Paper is defined as a matted or felted sheet usually composed of plant fibre. It has been made commercially for millennia, from sources as varied as linen, sugar cane, cotton and straw. Nowadays, it is almost exclusively made from cellulose fibre derived from wood. As well as being used as structural components of a wide array of packaging materials, especially for dry and ambient-stable foods, paper is used as an element in many other types of packaging, principally for labelling purposes.

With suitable coating, paperboards can withstand a range of temperatures and their stiffness provides protection to delicate contents. Paperboard is also used in combination with plastic laminates; it is an excellent light barrier, but its porosity means that gases can pass freely through it.

Paper and board have three basic properties in their favour: they are derived from renewable resources, are completely biodegradable, and are very easy to print on. Paper and board are non-specific terms that essentially refer to identical materials. They are usually distinguished either by their thickness or their weight: the International Standards Organisation states that material weighing 250gsm (g/m$^2$) or more shall be known as paperboard, but the paper industry uses the terms box board and carton board to describe heavier types of paper (Soroko, 1996).

Paper is usually a single-ply material, whereas board has a multi-ply structure. This multi-ply structure of board is a great advantage in the economical creation of different end products with different properties, by using different fibre types and densities in different layers. The ply structure, which comprises a mat of intermeshed cellulose fibres, is also important to the creasing and folding behaviour of boards. Maximum strength is achieved by processing long fibres, whereas maximum uniformity is achieved by using shorter, finer fibres.

**Manufacture of paper and board**

The principal source of paper and board fibre is conifer softwood, especially spruce and pine, but hardwoods (birch, aspen and eucalyptus), hemp, flax and jute are also used. The type of wood used significantly influences the physical properties of the end product. The conifers have cellulose fibres of about 3mm in length, which results in paper with high tensile and tear strengths. The hardwoods used typically have shorter fibres, which result in paper of lower physical strength. Linen fibres can be up to 55mm.

To make paper, it is necessary to break down the wood structure and separate the cellulose fibres. Once the bark has been stripped off, the wood contains about 40-45% cellulose and 5-10% hemicellulose, plus lignin. The wood is pulped by one of two methods: mechanical grinding or chemical digestion. Mechanical grinding is cheap, but does not remove the lignin and breaks the cellulose fibres, reducing their effective length and leading to a low-strength paper of poor uniformity. It is of limited use, although it can be added to bulk other pulps. Chemical digestion gives better quality, with virtually pure cellulose fibres. As the lignin and hemicellulose are dissolved away in the process, a yield of about 50% from the original wood is achieved. There are two principal chemical methods that can be used. The alkaline sulphate process is useful for soft woods and produces a neutral pulp of long, undamaged fibres, which gives rise to a strong paper, often referred to as kraft (German for strength). An alternative acidic sulphite process, although now in decline, is useful for producing finer papers, built up of shorter fibres. A combination of chemical and mechanical methods can be used to produce paper of intermediate quality, and thermomechanical methods can also be used (the wood is softened by heat before being mechanically refined).

Some of the properties of the final paper or board can be engineered in at this stage, by altering the degree of heating and chemical digestion of the pulp, or by the addition of other chemicals (see below). Physical treatments can also be applied to affect the properties of the final end product. For example, mechanical beating of pulp will cause cellulose fibres to fibrillate (split lengthways) and break. This results in fibre swelling and strong hydrogen bonding between the fibres, which then tend to consolidate. The fibrous nature of the paper is lost, and a 'greaseproof' paper results.

The mixture resulting from the pulping operation, known as 'furnish', is about 98% water, 1% cellulose fibres, and 1% other additives, and it is this that is fed to the paper making machine. Often, the furnish is not a single pulp type but a mixture, blended to yield paper of the desired properties. Among the additives that are added to the pulp are:

- sizing agents: to reduce the absorptivity of the paper, and improve its strength when wet. Untreated cellulose is essentially a highly absorbent blotting paper. Sizing agents, among other things, allow control of printing ink penetration on paper.

- bleaching agents: without bleaching agents, the colour of paper and pulp ranges from cream to light brown. Hydrogen peroxide, oxygen and chlorine-based bleaches are added to whiten the paper.

- biocides: in some applications, paper and board needs to be resistant to mould growth.

- coatings: clay, talc, titanium dioxide and similar materials can be included to achieve a finer, whiter surface finish, improving optical brightness and printing qualities (similar coatings can also be added to the dried paper - see below).

## Box 13 - Use of recycled paper

Recycled paper pulp is increasingly used. Although the furnish (the watery mixture resulting from the pulping operation) produced from recycled paper and board will have the properties of the original fibre source, each time the paper is recycled, fibres are degraded and their length is reduced, and the quality of the resultant paper is reduced. Recycled paper also contains many impurities, some of which cannot be removed, and which adversely affect the quality of the output. The use of recycled material is an important part of the paper and board industry and is increasing. Technology is continually being developed to overcome some of the limitations in quality that this poses.

There are several variations on how paper is actually made from the furnish. The two main methods are the cylinder method and the wire mesh method. In the former, a cylinder rotates in a vat of dilute pulp, and picks up most of the cellulose fibres via an array of small hooks on its surface. From the top of the cylinder, the web of paper is transferred to a continuous moving felt blanket, where it is transferred to dying and finishing sections. In the wire method, the web of paper is produced on a continuous moving fine wire mesh.

The paper web produced is very wet; it is weak and heavy and is easily distorted. It is left to dry naturally, and contracts significantly as a result. At this stage it will have a rough surface and will carry an imprint of the cylinder or wire. It is further dried by passing over a series of large heated cylinders, and ironed and smoothed out on heavy rolls - a process known as calendering. A shiny, glossy surface can also be produced at this stage by using a highly polished, heated metal drum.

The finished paper can be treated with a number of surface coatings. Starch and modified resins or waxes can be used to fill in surface voids and reduce liquid penetration rate. Clay, talc and titanium dioxide can be used to achieve a high standard of opacity, gloss and brightness

**Uses and requirements of paper and board**

Paper is widely used in the food industry as a material for labels on cans, jars and bottles, as well as a packaging material for dried foods like sugar and flour, and in combination with plastics in laminate composite packaging, such as Tetrapak packages for fruit juices and other liquid products. As a thin structural component on its own, it is prone to tearing or puncturing, but it has good burst strength, and it is best suited to enclosing relatively soft, uniform foods. It is very important to keep paper packages dry; although the materials used have a good enough moisture barrier to keep the contents dry in normal atmospheric conditions, long-term exposure to very moist atmospheres or direct contact with water will not be tolerated.

Flexible board is widely used for breakfast cereal boxes, and for other products that are contained within a flexible package, but which need some form of rigidity to both protect the foodstuff and allow it to be easily stacked and displayed. Cartons in this form also offer an ideal medium for presenting label information. Thicker, more rigid board is used in cylinders for packaging of crisps and other savoury snacks. Corrugated board is useful in general applications to provide a lightweight, but effective physical barrier to the environment.

Thicker forms of cardboard containers probably represent the biggest use of board - in the bulk packaging of items for transport from manufacturer to wholesaler and retailer.

**Box 14 - Carton board**

Carton board is paper with a weight above 250 g/m$^2$ or a thickness above 0.25mm. Boards manufactured for the production of cartons have a number of specific requirements to satisfy:

- good stiffness
- good printing surface
- good cutting, creasing and folding properties

The requirements of stiffness and folding are best satisfied by a low density board with large fibres, whereas a good printing surface is achieved with a finer, denser structure. However, this conflict is not a problem: as board is a multi-ply material, finer pulps are used for the surface plies, whereas stronger pulps are used for the centre plies.

There are many styles of cartons, with variations in shape and the way in which they are closed.

## 2.4 Plastic packaging

The development of plastics in general has revolutionised the food packaging industry. The versatility of plastics and the variety of characteristics that can be engineered-in mean that plastics can, in individual circumstances, replace all other packaging types, from thin paper bags, through transparent glass bottles and jars, to retortable rigid cans. They are generally lighter than most glass or metal containers (although aluminium cans are also very light), can be made transparent or opaque, and can vary from thin films through flexible bags to highly rigid bottles, depending on the particular need.

The term plastic is a rather loose expression - it is generally taken to mean a synthetic polymer made from simple organic chemical starting materials. Thermoset plastics were discovered in the 19th century; once moulded into the final form and set by heat they cannot be subsequently softened. The became relatively widely used

## Box 15 - Regenerated cellulose film

Regenerated cellulose film (RCF), or cellophane, was invented in France in the early 1900's and commercialised in the USA in 1924 by Du Pont. Although it is a polymer, cellophane is not a plastic, but it does have many characteristics that are similar plastics, and indeed it may be seen as the fore-runner to many plastics, having properties that have been subsequently engineered into different plastics. Many of these have contributed to the decline in the use of cellophane.

The word cellophane derives from cellulose and diaphane, meaning transparent. It is produced from high purity wood pulp, eucalyptus being often used. The pulp is soaked in sodium hydroxide solution for several hours to form alkali cellulose, which is then polymerised under controlled conditions (Jenkins, 1997). The cellulose fibres from the pulp are dissolved in carbon disulphide to form an alkali-soluble sodium cellulose xanthate, and this is then treated with dilute sodium hydroxide to form viscose, the main component of cellophane. A 'ripening period' of a few days then follows, after which the gelatinous material is extruded through a narrow slit onto a casting drum. The cellophane film is formed by coagulating the viscose in a solution of sulphuric acid and sodium sulphate. The film can then be washed and treated in various ways to yield products with specific characteristics useful for food packaging and other functions. For example, ethylene glycol or propylene glycol are incorporated to make it less brittle, and coatings of nitrocellulose or PVDC make it moisture proof.

In its early days, cellophane was an expensive, novelty packaging material, limited to the packaging of luxury items, but its adaptability and the variety of physical properties that could be engineered in soon widened its appeal, especially for baked goods and sweets. The advent of plastics such as polyethylene and polypropylene caused a decline in the market for cellophane, but it does have the advantage of being both biodegradable and manufactured from a renewable source. It also has some unique properties that continue to make it a viable product:

- Once shaped, it can maintain that shape - useful, for example for sweet wrappers
- It is relatively easy to tear
- Its glossy appearance can a 'premium' appearance for higher value products
- Its resistance to high temperatures is useful, for example, for hot-fill operations
- Coating with barrier resins can be a cheaper way of producing a packaging with high barrier properties than can be achieved with some coated plastic films

in the 1930s-1950s, Bakelite being the best known, but their brittleness and limitations on forming processes makes them unsuitable for most packaging containers. There are only three thermosets used to any extent in packaging: phenol-formaldehyde and urea-formaldehyde (which are both limited to applications such as some bottle closures), and glass-reinforced polyesters, which are used for large containers (Paine and Paine, 1983). Plastic food packaging is now dominated by thermoplastics, which can be subsequently shaped by heat.

There are many types of plastic polymers, each with their own specific characteristics, but within each class there is great scope for subtle modifications of their physical properties. As simple a property as the thickness of the material means that the same material can be used to produce wrapping films or rigid bottles.

### Box 16 - Brief glossary of some plastics terminology

Monomer - simple organic molecule that acts as a starting material for plastic

Polymer - long chain of monomer units joined chemically (often 10,000 units)

Homopolymer - polymer made from a single type of monomer (A), having the basic monomer structure A-A-A-A-A etc

Copolymer - polymer made from more than one starting monomer (A and B), with the monomers occurring in random order; e.g. A-A-B-A-B-B-A-B-B-B etc

Alternating copolymer - individual monomers alternate in the chain - can be considered as a homopolymer with an -AB- repeating unit, i.e. A-B-A-B-A-B-A etc

Block copolymer - a copolymer with long segments of one polymer followed by long segments of another copolymer. Properties intermediate between those of the respective homopolymers. Resemble polymer blends or alloys, but without the adhesion properties of these: e.g. A-A-A-A-B-B-B-B-A-A-A-A

Alloy - a mixture of two or more polymers (different from copolymer)

Plasticizer - an internal 'lubricant' added to increase polymer flexibility

Resin - polymer in its 'raw' state, before being formed into films, bottles etc

There is also considerable scope to mix different plastics starting materials to produce copolymers, further expanding the range and combination of properties that can be achieved. The nature of the plastic will determine what potential food packaging applications exist.

This section will look briefly at the characteristics of the major food packaging plastics, mentioning the points of most significance to each individual plastic, and at the techniques for actually physically producing the package from the 'raw' plastic material.

### Table 2 - Some major types of plastic food packaging and typical uses

High-density polyethylene - bottles
Low-density polyethylene - films and bags
Polypropylene - caps and closures
Polyvinyl chloride -bottles, stretch wrap, 'blister' packs
Polyethylene terephthalate - bottles
Polyvinylidene chloride - moisture barrier wraps
Nylons (polyamides) - cook-in bags
Polycarbonates - bottles
Polystyrene - cushioning and insulation

Plastic polymers are high-molecular-weight organic materials produced by combining highly purified simple organic molecules under controlled heat and pressure, usually in the presence of a catalyst or promoter. Although the starting materials for plastics are 10-50 times more expensive than ores and silica (the starting materials for metal and glass, respectively), the technology for plastic packaging material production has become so well developed that their cost-effectiveness is now well established (Throne, 1986). Chemically, polymers are generally formed by either addition reactions or condensation reactions. Both involve the addition of small molecules to a growing chain; in the latter, there is the concomitant release of a small molecule, such as water, during each reaction step (Selke, 1997).

Addition reaction example:   A + A ——>   A-A

Condensation reaction example: H-A + A-OH ——> A-A + $H_2O$

In this process, there are many opportunities for adding small quantities of other materials to alter the physicochemical properties of the polymer and its reaction to subsequent physical processing. Following production of the 'raw' plastic, it is then transformed into the many shapes, sizes and thicknesses that are demanded by modern food packaging needs.

As well as the basic monomer, a wide variety of additives are also used in polymer production to either improve the properties of the polymer or to remove unwanted 'side-effects'. Some of these are briefly described [see Rosato (1997) for more details]:

- Plasticisers are used to make a plastic more flexible and less brittle. Some plastics (e.g. PET bottles and thin polyethylene films) are flexible enough without the addition of plasticisers, but others such as PVC frequently require plasticisers in order to function in the desired way. Variation in the level of plasticiser added can allow a wide range of stiffnesses to be engineered into the polymer. Phthalic acid esters such as dioctyl phthalate are widely used for this function and act as external plasticisers (i.e. they are not incorporated into the polymer chain itself). Internal plasticisation can be achieved by copolymerising with other monomers. In all cases, the effect is to allow the polymer chains to move more easily relative to each other when a strain is applied.

- Colour - although many packaging polymers are unpigmented (especially when clarity is a major benefit), colourants are often added. The type of colourant that can be added will depend on the type of plastic, its end use and particularly on the degree of processing needed to reach the end product: for example, injection moulded polycarbonates require temperatures in excess of 300°C, and some pigments will degrade at these temperatures (Brody and Marsh, 1997). Some of the main colours used in plastics packaging are carbon black, titanium dioxide (white), iron oxide (red), cadmium sulphide (yellow), molybdate (orange), and copper phthalocyanines (blue and green).

- Lubricants are often incorporated to aid in processing the plastic into its final form. Plastics such as PVC, polyethylene and polypropylene tend to stick to metal parts during processing, and lubricants help to reduce this.

- Stabilizers - all plastics slowly degrade over time. Depending on the underlying cause, various chemicals can be incorporated to slow down the changes. These stabilisers can also help 'protect' the polymer during processing, when high temperatures and physical manipulations can also result in chemical degradation. Antioxidants are one group of stabilizing agents - butylated hydroxytoluene is a widely used example.

- Antifogging agents - fogging is a problem with some packaging film (especially if the product is still respiring). Antifogging agents such as hydrophilic fatty acid esters act by reducing surface tension, dispersing the water droplets and causing a continuous film of moisture to form.

The presence of these and other functional additives, along with unreacted monomers, catalysts and solvents in the final polymer mean that there is a significant potential for transfer of plastic packaging components into the food which it surrounds. This is closely controlled by legislation, which is described in Box 22 (page 62).

**The monomers**

*Polyethylene*

Polyethylene (or polythene), the most widely used plastic packaging in the world, is formed by the addition polymerisation of ethylene (ethene). This involves the breaking of the double bond in individual ethylene molecules and joining the individual units together in a long chain, thus:

$$n \times H_2C = CH_2 \longrightarrow -(H_2C\text{-}CH_2)_n^-$$

In high-density polyethylene (HDPE), an essentially linear chain molecule is formed. In low-density polyethylene (LDPE) a branched structure is created. The degree of chain branching can be varied, so that there is no chemical definition of where HDPE ends and LDPE begins. However, the polyethylene industry generally terms HDPE as being 0.94 g/cm$^3$ and above. The degree of branching effectively inhibits the chains from crystallizing, so keeping the chains apart and making the polymer less dense.

ICI was the first company to produce LDPE, in 1933, by applying high pressures to ethylene gas at high temperatures. Current high pressure processes utilise small amounts of an initiator, typically oxygen or peroxide, to start the polymerisation process. The precise characteristics of the final product, such as average molecular weight, molecular weight distribution and density - which are related to the degree of branching and overall chain length of the polymer - are controlled by the reaction temperature, ethylene pressure and the concentration of chain-transfer reagents (Maraschin, 1986).

The development of HDPE followed that of LDPE in the 1950's when three research groups independently came up with low-pressure systems for making polyethylene, utilising metal catalyst-based systems. The two systems which have been developed as the major HDPE producing systems worldwide are based on chromium oxide/silica and metal halide/aluminium alkyl catalysts (Smith, 1986).

Low-pressure processes were commercialised in the 1970s for producing LDPE-type polymers. In these, the branching characteristics are achieved by copolymerisation with co-monomers such as 1-butene, 1-hexene or 1-octene, which act like short-chain branches, although the main polymer itself is a straight-chain (linear) molecule. This type of polymer is usually referred to as linear LDPE (LLDPE). Incorporating higher co-monomer levels results in the production of very-low-density polyethylene (VLDPE). More recently, the use of metallocene catalysts has increased the manufacturer's control over polyethylene structure, allowing the production of long chain branches in otherwise linear polymers. Metallocene catalysts are based on a metal atom such as titanium, zirconium or hafnium attached to carbon-based moieties such as cyclopentadienyl groups.

The ability to vary the degree and length of branching, the polymer chain length and other properties allows a whole range polyethylene products to be formed, so that it is suitable for a wide variety of food packaging functions. It is a non-polar plastic, making it a relatively good barrier to water vapour and other polar materials. Because of its higher crystallinity and lower amorphous areas (where permeation of polar materials occurs) HDPE is a better barrier than LDPE. However, neither are good barriers to oxygen or carbon dioxide, nor are they effective barriers against hydrocarbon-based compounds. The non-polar nature of the polyethylene surface also makes it difficult to print on, so for labelling purposes, the surface usually has to be treated in some way.

## Box 17 - Polar and non-polar molecules

Many of the properties of plastic polymers are dependent on the degree of polarity or otherwise of the molecule. Atoms can be thought of as being made up of a positively charged nucleus, surrounded by negatively charged electrons. Molecules are a collection of atoms joined together. In many cases, the subatomic structure of the molecule means that the distribution of positive and negative charge is uneven - in simple terms the electrons are pulled away from one atom towards another, resulting in a polar molecule, one end of the molecule being positively charged, while the other end is negatively charged. This is a very common occurrence throughout the biological and chemical world. For example, in the water molecule, the oxygen atom tends to pull electrons towards itself and away from the hydrogen atoms, resulting in a negatively charged oxygen atom and positively charged hydrogen atoms: a polar molecule. In contrast, in long-chain hydrocarbon molecules, consisting of carbon-carbon and carbon-hydrogen bonds, there is no such charge distribution. Plastics may consist almost entirely of non-polar chains, or may also have polar side groups. Polar molecules tend to associate with each other, and not with non-polar molecules. Water is the most significant polar molecule with regard to the properties of plastics - it will be repelled by non-polar plastics, but not by polar plastics.

At room temperature, polyethylene is a fairly soft and flexible material. Because of this it is not always suitable for caps and closures, as it can be deformed by external pressures to an unacceptable degree, resulting in seals being broken. It maintains its properties of softness at low temperatures and is therefore well suited to frozen food packaging. However, around 100°C it becomes too soft for many uses (Selke, 1997).

HDPE is most widely used for large-volume containers such as milk bottles, because of its low cost and ease of forming. Although it has a translucent appearance, and so is not suitable for packaging that requires a high degree of clarity, it can be easily pigmented. LDPE is more flexible than HDPE and is generally too soft for most types of bottle, but it is suitable for films and bags because of its low cost. Although clearer than HDPE, it is still not suitable for applications than require complete transparency.

*Polypropylene*

Polypropylene is formed by the addition polymerisation of propylene:

$$n \times CH_2 = CH\text{-}CH_3 \longrightarrow \text{-}(CH_2\,CH)_n\text{-}$$
$$|$$
$$CH_3$$

Typically, 1,000-30,000 propylene molecules are combined in a single polymer chain. Its chemical properties (e.g. poor resistance to organic chemicals) are fairly similar to those of polyethylene, but it has several different physical properties.

One of the main ways in which the properties of polypropylene can be controlled is in the orientation of the methyl ($CH_3$) group. The end of the propylene molecule with three hydrogen atoms is called the head. If, on polymerisation, the molecules are joined head-to-head and head-to-tail randomly in about equal amounts, the resulting polymer has little order and does not crystallise. This is termed atactic or amorphous polypropylene, which is soft, tacky and soluble in many solvents, making it suitable for hot-melt adhesives. If the polymers are connected head-to-tail almost every time, a crystalline polymer results, called isotactic polypropylene, which is solvent- and heat-resistant and stiff (Miller, 1986). Syndiotactic polypropylene can also be produced, with the methyl groups on alternate sides of the chain, but this has no significant use in packaging (Selke, 1997).

Polypropylene has a lower density than most polyethylenes (except for VLDPE), as the methyl group in the polymer chain causes the structure to be looser. The methyl group also interferes with the rotation of the main polymer chain, causing the material to be stiffer. This property means that polypropylene is widely used in caps and closures, as it is not so easily deformed as, say, polyethylene. It is also very tolerant of repeated flexing, so making it suitable for hinged closures that are repeatedly opened and closed.

Polypropylene, like polyethylene, is a good barrier to water vapour, but a poor barrier to oxygen and carbon dioxide. It has a higher melting point than polyethylene and is useful for microwaveable packaging and hot-filled bottles (where HDPE becomes too soft), but it becomes brittle at low temperatures. If it is to be used in frozen food packaging, a small amount of ethylene co-monomer (typically 1-5%) is incorporated into the polymerisation mixture. The resultant copolymers have lower and broader melting points than the homopolymer. They are also relatively clear.

As well as uses in closures, polypropylene is used for bottle manufacture - the new generation of metallocene catalysts has further enhanced the material's transparency, improving its usefulness for this purpose. Polypropylene films also have good transparency and are used as sweet wrappers and snack food pouches, and have replaced cellophane in a number of applications (Miller, 1986).

*Polyvinyl chloride*

Polyvinyl chloride (PVC) is an addition polymer of vinyl chloride (i.e. one formed by an addition reaction):

$$n \times CH_2 = CHCl \longrightarrow -(CH_2CHCl)_n-$$

It is one of a number of polymers based on the vinyl moiety; others include polyvinyl alcohol, polyvinylidene chloride, polyvinyl fluoride and polyvinyl acetate. The versatility of the polymerisation process means that there is a wide range of copolymers that can be produced.

When first developed, it was almost impossible to process 'raw' PVC resin into usable products without thermal degradation - its melting point is very close to its decomposition temperature, and it yields hydrogen chloride when it decomposes.

However, the addition of stabilisers and plasticisers enables a wide range of properties to be engineered into PVC. The polar nature of the C-Cl bond in PVC means that it has high affinity for plasticisers and other additives, allowing the production of PVC with a wide range of stiffness. It is probably the most versatile of plastics in use in the food packaging industry.

PVC is normally polymerised from its monomer in an exothermic reaction (i.e. one which gives out heat energy) at 35-75°C in the presence of peroxide-type initiators (Cocco, 1986). Four different processes are used in PVC production, and these allow the production of PVC resin with different characteristics.

PVC has good transparency, with a slightly bluish tint. It yellows with age and is therefore sometimes tinted a more pronounced blue as this tends to mask the yellowing effect. PVC has been widely used as a food wrap. It has good self-clinging properties, allowing good sealability, and its oxygen permeability means that it is especially suited to wrap fresh meat, as it allows the meat's red colour and appearance of freshness to be maintained. Rigid PVC is also used for bottles for milk, honey and edible oils.

Despite its technical versatility, the use of PVC in general has recently been inhibited by both environmental and health concerns. The disposal of PVC is a problem: when burnt it emits hydrogen chloride, and it may contribute to the formation of environmental chlorinated dioxins. There are also general concerns about the fate and effects of chlorinated organic compounds in the environment.

Specific food contact concerns centre around the migration of vinyl chloride monomers from the polymer into the food. During the polymerisation process, there is incomplete conversion of the monomer into polymer, resulting in monomer being still present in the final resin product. These can be transferred to food fairly readily, especially to foods with a high fat content (such as cheese), and there is evidence that vinyl chloride can be carcinogenic under some circumstances (Selke, 1997). Legislation generally limits the amount of any monomer that can be transferred to food (via the Plastic Materials and Articles in Contact with Food Regulations see Box 22, page 62). Manufacturers of PVC responded to the potential problem of vinyl chloride transfer by drastically reducing the amount of vinyl chloride monomer in the polymer, by subjecting it to repeated applications of a vacuum.

Despite this, there has been a general move away from the use of PVC films for certain food wrap applications in the UK.

**Polyethylene terephthalate (PET)**

PET is the most widely used of a group of polymers called polyesters, which have the general formula:

$$\text{HO-(CO-R-CO-R'-O)}_n\text{-H}$$

Where R and R' are various organic groups (Selke, 1997).

PET is formed by the condensation polymerisation of terephthalic acid and ethylene glycol (in which water molecules are formed), or ethylene glycol and the dimethyl ester of terephthalic acid (in which methanol is the condensation side-product).

$$\text{nHOOC-C}_6\text{H}_4\text{-COOH} \quad + \quad \text{nHOCH}_2\text{CH}_2\text{OH}$$
(Terephthalic acid)         (ethylene glycol)

$$\downarrow$$

$$\text{HOCH}_2\text{CH}_2\text{-[OOC-C}_6\text{H}_4\text{-COOCH}_2\text{CH}_2]_n\text{-OH}$$

(PET)

This is essentially a two-stage reaction. Heating the monomers initially forms a short chain polymer, which is viscous molten liquid. It is extruded and water-quenched to form a glass-like amorphous material. A second polymerisation stage, under vacuum at around 285°C, is then performed on the dried and crystallised resin chips. Very low concentrations of catalysts are used to promote the process and make it commercially viable. Antimony trioxide is the most commonly used, but salts of titanium, germanium, cobalt, manganese, magnesium and zinc are also used and small amounts remain encapsulated in the polymer matrix or in the polymer chain itself (ILSI, 2000). Once formed, the polymer is very difficult to purify, and so a high degree of purity in the starting materials is required.

The crystallinity of PET can be manipulated to make it useful for different food packaging applications. When heated above 72°C it changes from a rigid glass-like state into a rubbery elastic form. Aligning the polymer chains in two directions and then cooling them quickly while the chains are still in the stretched state 'freezes' the chains, resulting in a material that is suitable for forming films and bottles. Holding the polymer at 72°C and allowing it to slowly crystallise results in the material becoming opaque, more rigid and less flexible. This form can withstand higher temperatures, making it suitable for use as ovenable trays.

The toughness of uncrystallised PET in relation to its weight and its similarity to glass regarding transparency means that it has become widely used in bottles for soft drinks. It also is a better barrier to oxygen and carbon dioxide than PVC, polypropylene and polyethylene, meaning that it is particularly suitable for carbonated drinks, where it has largely replaced glass. Incorporating isophthalic acid co-monomer in the manufacture of PET allows the manufacture of thicker bottle walls, sheets and films (ILSI, 2000). This type of PET is also used to make wide-mouth jars and tubs for jams and similar products.

Crystallised PET can be used as trays for pre-cooked and/or frozen ready meals, and can be reheated in either conventional or microwave ovens, while PET products with an added oxygen barrier have use in vacuum-packed dairy products and 'bag-in-box' wines amongst others (see ILSI, 2000 for a list of PET applications).

PET is perceived as an 'environment friendly' material, and is relatively simple to recycle and re-use. It also appears to have no significant adverse health implications, and its low diffusion coefficient means that it is difficult for contaminants to diffuse either in or out of the material.

A related plastic is polyethylene naphthalate (PEN), a condensation polymer of ethylene glycol and naphthalate dicarboxylate. Amongst its improved properties, compared to PET, are:

- better barrier to oxygen and water vapour
- higher tensile strength
- better chemical resistance

- greater resistance to hydrolysis
- UV barrier
- High temperature resistance, allowing hot filling of bottles

However, it is several times more expensive than PET and is likely to be limited to applications in PEN/PET copolymers.

**Polystyrene**

Polystyrene is an addition polymer of styrene:

$$n \times C_6H_5\text{-}CH = CH_2 \longrightarrow \text{-}(C_6H_5\text{-}CH\text{-}CH_2)_n\text{-}$$

Most polystyrene is produced by solution polymerisation, which is a continuous process catalysed by organic peroxides and hydroperoxides, such as benzoyl peroxide. In this, styrene and solvent pass through a series of reactors, from which unreacted styrene and the solvent are removed and recycled, and molten polymer is cooled and pelletised. In an alternative process, the suspension process, the styrene monomer is dispersed in water with a suspending agent and the mixture is heated in a closed vessel until polymerisation is substantially complete (ILSI, 2002).

In the polymer, the benzene rings are randomly ordered, resulting in atactic polystyrene, which is unable to crystallise. The large benzyl side groups also cause considerable resistance to chain rotation, and polystyrene is resultantly a highly stiff, brittle material. Its non-crystalline nature also makes it highly transparent. It also begins to flow at around 100°C, and so is not suitable for use at high temperatures, but this property means that it is easy to extrude and thermoform. This type of polystyrene ('crystal' polystyrene) is used when a completely clear product is required, such as for disposable 'plastic glasses' for drinks.

These are very different properties to the lightweight, opaque packaging foam material that is so familiar - foamed or expanded polystyrene. This is produced by incorporating a volatile expanding agent, typically a hydrocarbon (usually pentane or butane) or more recently carbon dioxide, into the molten polymer. Chlorofluorocarbons used to be used for this purpose, but were phased out following the Montreal Protocol agreement to restrict the use of ozone-depleting substances. Carbon dioxide has several advantages - it is not flammable, does not result in volatile organic compound emissions (although it is a 'greenhouse' gas), and confers properties that make the final polystyrene product less prone to taint foods, so that it can be used with a wider range of products. Foamed polystyrene is used in many food packaging situations - as trays for retail sale of meats, fish and other foods, in egg boxes (where its cushioning properties are very useful), as 'fast-food' containers, and as disposable cups for drinks. In all of these situations, its very light weight (typically $0.05$-$0.19 g/cm^3$) is a major advantage. In some cases the foam polystyrene has a surface layer of crystal polystyrene to act as the food/packaging interface.

A third form of polystyrene is high-impact polystyrene (HIPS). This is an opaque material, in which butadiene rubber is incorporated. At the start of the polymerisation process, polybutadiene rubber is dissolved into the styrene monomer. As the process proceeds, some styrene monomers react with the rubber, resulting in the polybutadiene being grafted onto the polystyrene. As well as reducing the clarity of the polystyrene, it also makes it much less brittle. HIPS are used as vending cups for beverages and also as tubs for refrigerated dairy products, often in blends with crystal polystyrene.

**Nylon**

People tend to associate nylon with clothing, but there are many types of nylon used in food and other packaging. The name derives from the fact that it was first produced in New York and London.

Nylons are a group of polyamide polymers, formed from carboxylic acid and amide-containing monomers. They can either be produced from mixtures of dicarboxylic acids and diamines,

$$nH_2NR^1NH_2 + nHOOCR^2COOH \longrightarrow H(NHR^1NHCOR^2CO)_nOH$$

or from amino acids

$$nH_2NR^3COOH \longrightarrow H(NHR^3CONHR^3CO)_nOH$$

(where the R groups are carbon chains)

Nylons are identified by a numbering system which identifies the number of carbon atoms in the starting monomers. Thus, nylon 6,10 is formed from a diamine containing 6 carbon atoms and a dicarboxylic acid containing 10 carbon atoms, and nylon 11 is formed from an amino acid containing 11 carbon atoms.

The variety of starting materials, in combination with variations in production and processing conditions, means that a whole family of polymers can be produced to meet a variety of needs. Generally, they have good thermal stability and low temperature flexibility, and are good barriers to volatile flavours and odours, gases and oils. Increasing the number of carbon atoms in the chain between the CONH groups tends to lower the melting point, tensile strength and water absorption of the nylon, while increasing its elongation and impact strength (Selke, 1997). The high strength and toughness can be further enhanced by orientation - aligning the polymer chains so that they pack more tightly. This also enhances barrier properties (Tubridy and Sibilia, 1986). Nylon-6 has been the type most frequently used in packaging applications, because of its overall superiority in terms of cost, physical properties and process adaptability.

Nylons are generally more expensive than other plastics, but they can perform specific roles in packaging that make the additional cost worthwhile. Typical uses are in 'cook-in' bags, cheese packaging, vacuum packaging of bacon and other meats, and modified atmosphere packaging

**Other polymers**

The polymers already mentioned give a good overall impression of the variety of properties that can be engineered into the final material. The variability in rigidity, heat and cold sensitivity, gas and water vapour permeability, and transparency, amongst other properties of single polymers, copolymers and polymer blends allow the food packager and packaging manufacturer a variety of choices for a particular function. Other considerations to be born in mind include costs of each plastic and, as will be discussed later, the ease of actually forming the final package shape.

In addition to the polymers described above, there are many others also available, and brief descriptions of some of these are detailed below.

*Polycarbonate*

The full name for this is poly(bisphenol-A carbonate), and has the structure:

$$H-[O-Ph-C(CH_3)_2-Ph-OCO)_n-OH$$

(where Ph is a phenyl ($C_6H_5$) group)

It is an amorphous (non-crystalline) polymer and is very clear, with a light transmittance value very close to that of clear, plate glass (Mihalich and Baccaro, 1986). It is very tough and rigid, and exhibits resistance to both high and low temperatures. Its wide softening range (i.e. it does not have a clearly defined melting point) help to make it very easy to form into shapes. These properties have led to it being used almost exclusively now in place of glass for refillable water bottles and similar items.

*Polyvinylidene chloride (PVDC)*

This is an addition polymer of vinylidene chloride, with the following structure:

$$-(CH_2CCl_2)_n-$$

Like PVC, it tends to decompose at high temperatures. Combined with its highly crystalline nature (in contrast to PVC), this makes it very difficult to process, and it is usually copolymerised with other monomers such as vinyl chloride, methyl acrylate and methyl methacrylate. The main property of PVDC is as a barrier to moisture, gases (particularly oxygen), and volatile flavour constituents of foods, and so is very effective as household food wrap (it has excellent 'cling' properties). In copolymerising with other monomers, the main aim is to improve its ease of processing without unduly compromising these barrier characteristics. It is often used as a coating on other packaging materials to give the materials these added characteristics. However, it is an organochlorine-based molecule, like PVC, and so environmental issues have to be taken into consideration.

*Polyvinyl acetate*

This is an atactic (i.e. unarranged), amorphous addition polymer of vinyl acetate. It is tough and relatively stiff at room temperature, but softens and becomes sticky with a small increase in temperature. Its main use in packaging is as an adhesive, especially for paper; the polar nature of the acetate group enhancing its ability to bind substances together.

*Poly(ethylene-vinyl alcohol) (EVOH)*

EVOH is one of the more important copolymers used in food packaging. Poly(vinyl alcohol) has exceptionally high gas-barrier properties, but it is water-soluble and difficult to process. By copolymerising vinyl alcohol with ethylene, the high gas-barrier properties are retained and improvements are achieved in moisture resistance and processability (Foster, 1986). EVOH has recently been used in a number of applications, in conjunction with other polymers.

*Ionomers*

Ionomers are polymers that contain interchain ionic bonding. They were discovered by the Du Pont company in the 1960s, when producing highly branched low density polyethylene copolymers with methacrylic acid, using a high-pressure process. Neutralizing the polymers with either sodium or zinc was found to result in a

## Box 18  - Combination of polymers

There are four basic techniques for combining polymers in layers:

- co-extrusion for films or tubes - two or more plastics are extruded from separate bulk areas through one die
- co-injection moulding for containers - two or more plastics are injected in measured quantities into a mould
- lamination - preformed plastics are joined in layers in some way
- coating - one preformed plastic is coated with another

In all cases, the intention is to combine different polymers with different properties in order to get the best combination of characteristics at least cost. For example, polypropylene is a relatively low cost plastic suitable for food contact, which has excellent water vapour barrier properties as well as good heat and impact resistance. However, it is a poor oxygen barrier, and so is unsuitable for packaging oxygen-sensitive foods requiring a long shelf life. On the other hand, polyethylene vinyl alcohol has excellent oxygen barrier properties, but is a more expensive plastic. It is also sensitive to water and so is not ideal for contact with foods with any significant water content. The ideal solution is to incorporate a thin layer of polyethylene vinyl alcohol between two layers of polypropylene. This can be achieved by either extrusion or injection-moulding techniques. In co-injection, 2 units would operate in one mould, delivering metered amounts of plastic to form a parison, which can subsequently be blow-moulded. Both this and co-extrusion rely on the laminar flow properties of polymers, i.e. their tendency to flow in layers, and not to mix with each other.

As well as being combined with each other, plastics are frequently combined with metal or paper/board or both. Metallizing (see box 19) is one specific application, but laminate composites with metal foil and board are becoming increasingly widespread: these are used in packages for heat-sterilised, long-life products such as fruit juices and soft drinks, ready-to-serve custard and similar liquid-based aseptically processed products.

product with distinctly different properties. The polymer was found to contain ionic regions in addition to the crystalline and amorphous (non-crystalline) regions present on polyethylene.

Ionomers have similar properties to LDPE, but have higher toughness and tensile strength, greater clarity, a lower softening point (which helps in forming packaging), greater abrasion resistance and better oil resistance (Longworth, 1986).

**Shaping plastics into packaging materials**

The previous sections have described the basics of making plastic polymers, but these are not in themselves the final packaging material (just as a plate of glass is not a bottle and sheet metal is not a can). One of the great advantages of plastics, besides the variety of starting materials, is the many forms into which they can be manufactured: trays, bottles and jars, and various types and thicknesses of films. There are different techniques for achieving these end products; procedures will be modified depending on the type of plastic involved.

### Box 19 - Combination of plastics - metallizing

Metallizing of plastic is one specific example of the combination of plastics with other materials. In this, a very thin layer of metal (usually aluminium) is coated on to the plastic (the thickness is about 300 times less than thin commercial foils), usually to improve the barrier properties of clear products. This operation is achieved by melting and vapourising the aluminium in a vacuum chamber (as low as 3.1kPa pressure - 0.9 in. of mercury) and spraying it onto the plastic, which is usually in the form of a roll of film. The amount of metal on the plastic is controlled by the temperature of the aluminium (the hotter it is, the more metal is deposited), the running speed of the plastic film through the chamber and the number of plating stations (application points) within the chamber. This process tends to improve the inherent barrier properties in the original plastic film, rather than confer additional properties. For example, the good oxygen barrier properties of biaxially oriented nylon film are significantly improved, but the poor water barrier properties are not materially affected. In contrast, the good moisture barrier properties of biaxially oriented polypropylene film are significantly enhanced (Prince, 1986).

There are several ways in which plastic containers (e.g. bottles and jars) can be formed:

- Injection moulding: the raw material is softened in a heated cylinder. When it is sufficiently fluid, it is then forced under high pressure into a closed, relatively cold mould. The plastic takes the shape of the mould, and when cooled the mould is opened and the container is removed. Multi-cavity moulds can be used with this technique, and high production rates can be achieved. However, the moulds are expensive and so short runs are not economic. Also, there is a limit to the shapes that can be achieved with this method, because of the difficulty in removing them from the mould.

- Rotational moulding: finely ground powder is heated in a rotating mould until it melts or fuses. The inner surface of the mould is uniformly coated, and the whole is allowed to cool before the formed contained is removed.

- Blow moulding: in commercial practice there are two types of blow moulding methods - injection blowing and extrusion blowing. In injection blowing, the plastic material is moulded around a blowing stick inside an injection moulding machine. As in glass container manufacturing, this results in the formation of a thick-walled tube called a parison. The parison and the blowing stick are transferred to a blowing mould and compressed air is passed down the stick to blow the parison into the shape of the mould. In extrusion blowing, the parison is derived from a continuously extruded tube. Lengths of the tube are trapped between two halves of a split mould, the ends are closed as the mould closes, and the trapped parison is blown into the shape of the mould by compressed air.

- Stretch blow moulding: unless 'persuaded' to behave otherwise, the polymer chains in a plastic will coil together and be arranged in a completely random fashion. Stretch blow moulding (or biaxial-orientation blow moulding) is a way of achieving a specific alignment of the molecules to give specific properties to the plastic, particularly enhancing stiffness, impact strength, surface gloss, transparency and barrier properties. The enhanced strength properties means that thinner, lighter containers can be produced. Polypropylene and especially PET (for carbonated beverage bottles) can be formed in this way. The critical step is the heating of a preform or parison to a specific temperature (usually just above the glass transition temperature) and rapidly stretching and cooling it in a mould, in order to align the polymer molecules.

- Thermoforming: in this process, plastic sheet is softened by heat and then either forced into or over a mould, using compressed air, a vacuum or both. The container is then punched out of the sheet and trimmed, and pieces of waste plastic are recycled. This is a very versatile method and a variety of shapes and sizes of container can be produced in this way. Shallow trays are regularly produced in this way.

## Box 20 - The emergence of semi-rigid plastic packaging
(see Campbell 1991)

The production of food in semi-rigid plastic containers, that require a heat treatment to achieve long-term stability under ambient storage conditions, has emerged over the past 15 years, as an addition to the traditional can, offering additional benefits of presentation and convenience for premium quality food products. Typical containers are a rigid pot or tray with a flexible metal or plastic foil lid. Modern automatic processing systems have greatly enhanced the uses to which manufacturers can put this type of package. The containers are manufactured from combinations of thermoplastics, sometimes with other materials added to give additional properties. A detailed technical performance specification will be required to ensure that the package is suitable for the food it contains and the process it will be subjected to.

As with canning systems, the packaging has to be protected from damage which could give rise to loss of container integrity and subsequent microbial contamination; for the same reason, the filling and sealing operations have to be carefully controlled, and the fill weight is particularly important. After heat processing, the containers have to be rapidly cooled to about 45°C, and the pressure within them has to be controlled to prevent undue stress on the lid seams.

All-plastic containers have found a major niche in microwave reheating, as metal is not generally suitable for use in microwave ovens. This has extended the role of this type of packaging to chilled and frozen ready meals, requiring only a pasteurisation or cooking step, rather than a full sterilisation process.

As well as being formed into containers, plastic resins can be converted to thin films. These are produced by melting the plastic resin in a hopper and extruding the result through a die, which has a thin, wide cross-section to its exit. Immediately it exits the die, the plastic is cooled on quenching rollers to below its melting point, and is thus solidified into its desired shape and thickness. By controlling the speed of the quenching rollers at slightly more than the film exits the die, the film can be stretched as it cools. This allows thinner films to be produced, but also results in alignment of the polymer molecules, thus conferring enhanced toughness, stiffness and film clarity in the same way as is achieved in stretch blow moulding of containers.

One of the advantages of some plastics is that they can be blown or moulded on site, therefore large packaging stores are not necessarily required, as they usually are for cans, bottles and glass.

# 3. FUNCTIONS OF PACKAGING

The main functions of food packaging are to deliver the product to the consumer (or the intermediate customer, such as a caterer or food manufacturer) in its desired state, to inform the consumer the nature of the contents, and to do these things in a way convenient to the consumer. Thus, packaged raw meat needs to be packed so that juices do not run out, carbonated beverages must reach their destination still carbonated, and large packages should not be unnecessarily heavy. In addition, the package may also serve an additional function after it has been opened (e.g. it may be resealable). Many specific issues are dealt with elsewhere in this book: this short chapter merely states in general terms what the major roles of packaging are.

## Physical protection

There are two main way in which packaging affords physical/mechanical protection to products: via primary packaging (that which actually encloses the product) and via secondary packaging (boxes and crates, etc. that enclose the primary packages). Most products are distributed in large quantities and adequate protection is required to resist the damage that might occur in handling, storage and transport. In some cases it is the product itself that might become damaged, in others it is the primary packaging that must be protected.

Dry, friable products such as crisps, cereals and bakery products need some sort of primary packaging that will protect the food and prevent slight to moderate crush damage - i.e. stop the crisps or cereal flakes from being reduced to a powder, or prevent the cakes from being reduced to crumbs. In general, crisp packets achieve this by being filled with a slight overpressure of gas (a modified atmosphere that also serves to prolong shelf life by retarding the loss of crispness and the onset of rancidity). Breakfast cereals, cakes and similar products are contained in a paperboard packaging that offers resistance to physical damage.

All products need to be protected from the greater physical abuse that might befall them during storage and transport. Clearly, the primary packaging will not be able to prevent damage that might be caused by fork-lift trucks, or stacking on warehouse shelving. Sturdy cardboard boxes or plastic crates are usually required for this. Apart from the obvious damage that might occur to foods packaged in paperboard or flexible plastic, and the potential breakage of glass or rigid plastic packages themselves, the hidden, minor damage that can occur to packages must also be considered. For example, the purpose of packaging food in hermetically sealed metal cans is to maintain it, after processing, in a sterile environment. Deforming the cans in any way can either distort the lid or side seals or result in pinholes in the body of the can, both of which could allow microorganisms to enter the product, thus negating the sterilisation process. Similarly, products packed in a modified atmosphere, whose shelf life relies on a specific gas mixture surrounding the product, will be compromised if the seal of the package is broken or if any of the packaging is punctured (the film lid would be the most susceptible).

### Prevention of contamination

Packaging must be designed to prevent unwanted physical, chemical and micro-biological contamination of the food enclosed, for both quality and safety reasons. Some contaminants may not affect the appearance or taste of the product, but be a hazard to health; other contaminants may be quite innocuous from a health point of view, but detract from the acceptability of the food, in some cases making it inedible.

Prevention of physical damage, as discussed above, is one prerequisite for the prevention of contamination. However, to prevent microbial contamination, seals, lids and closures also need to be appropriately constructed. Assuming that the package does not itself adversely pass material to the food, this will also prevent chemical and physical contamination. For packages that do not need to be hermetically sealed for shelf stability, such as dried foods, where microbial contamination is not a major issue, there is still a need for packages to be designed so that foreign bodies cannot gain entry. This may be as simple as a piece of debris falling into open bottle or jar, but a more specific example is of mites or other small organisms getting into packets of flour, rice and similar products. Many of these packages are now being fitted with adhesive resealing tabs to prevent this.

Also commonplace now on many packages are 'tamper-evident' devices, such as foil seals, which indicate whether a package has been opened (see section 5.3).

As well as preventing contamination from outside, the packaging itself must not contaminate the product. This requirement is controlled by the two pieces of 'Materials and Articles' legislation noted in box 22 (page 62).

## Control of internal changes

There are many ways in which packaging controls changes that might occur to a food during storage. The simplest of these is possibly moisture loss. Even packages that are not vapour tight offer a good level of protection against moisture loss. This is true for foods as diverse as fresh and cooked fish and meat, and cakes and bakery products. For products such as fresh fruit and vegetables, the opposite effect is a problem - the products continue to respire and produce water, so the package will usually be designed to allow this to escape in some way. Other foods might pick up moisture from the surrounding atmosphere over time (dry foods may become soft, and powdered foods might become 'caked'). In these cases, special moisture absorbers may be incorporated into the package to prevent or delay this (see section 5.2 on active packaging). The role of tin in metal cans on the maintenance of food quality characteristics has been discussed in chapter 2 - this is another, traditional form of active packaging.

Two major types of changes that can occur in packaged foods are microbial and chemical spoilage. As described in section 5.1 on modified atmosphere packaging, this can be slowed by the use of appropriate packaging.

Carbonated beverages need to maintain their level of carbonation until the packaging is initially opened. Consideration then has to be paid as to whether the drink will be consumed in one go, or whether a resealable package is required.

**Consumer information**

Packaging has a vital role to play in informing the customer about the contents of food. Information on packaging can be divided into two broad categories: advertising and related information, and legally required factual information. In fact, there is a great deal of overlap between these two categories, as much of the advertising on food packaging is controlled by legislation. Food must be labelled in such a way that the customer can make an informed choice as to whether to buy it or not.

Harmonised legislation throughout the European Community, enacted in Great Britain as The Food Labelling Regulations 1996, as amended, prescribes many requirements for a food label. These can have a significant effect on decisions made regarding the nature of the packaging used - e.g. the use of an 'overwrap' or extra packaging in multi-pack products.

All food must have a clear product name, and a supplementary description if a 'fancy' name is used; e.g. 'MiniRolls', where 'MiniRoll' is the fancy name, will have a supplementary description along the lines of: "Individual milk chocolate covered swiss roll with vanilla flavour filling"." Also usually required are a weight or volume or number marking, a list of ingredients, storage, cooking or reheating instructions, if appropriate, an indication of shelf-life ('use by' or 'best before'), company details relating to the manufacturer, packer or seller of the food (and sometimes the geographical origin of the food itself - such as New Zealand cheddar), and in some cases, data describing the nutritional content of the food. Although nutrition information is not obligatory unless a nutrition claim (such as low-fat or high-fibre) is made on the label, its provision has become widespread. In some cases, this can result in space constraints on the packaging.

Various warning statements are also either obligatory or recommended/voluntary in certain situations (e.g. 'contains a source of phenylalanine' for products containing the artificial sweetener aspartame, or 'contains nuts'). Recently, a need to quantify the amount of certain ingredients in some products has been introduced - the so-called QUID (Quantitative Ingredients Declaration) regulations.

Some of these requirements need to be in the same field of vision. This itself puts constraints on the nature and size of the packaging used. Although there is no prescriptive requirements for the size and nature of typeface - except for the quantity market - used in package label information, there is an over-riding requirement that it is legible, and so there is a limit to how small a package surface area can be.

In addition to factual information, the label must not give misleading information, e.g. through misleading pictorial representation, or be so badly presented as to make the true nature of the information difficult to ascertain. In some situations, the nature of the packaging may influence what needs to be disclosed on the label. Being able to see the product through the packaging may sometimes mean that certain information does not need to be given.

On top of the legally required information, the food manufacturer will want to make the product look as attractive as possible, e.g. by including suggestions for recipes including the product enclosed. The use of clear packaging (e.g. glass or plastic jars for brightly coloured products) may be desirable in some cases.

## Box 21 - Food labelling advice from the Food Standards Agency

Recently, the UK Food Standards Agency has issued advice to industry on how labelling could be improved to ensure that consumers are able to find information easily and understand how to use it. The advice covers: the grouping of information, the formats of nutrition labelling and date marking (i.e. an indication of shelf-life), allergens and ingredient listing, print size and clarity, and increasing the printable area of the pack. This latter opinion is probably the most significant for those involved in food packaging design, although all the points raised may have some impact. The main recommendations are that labels should:

- Group key facts together, such as 'use by' information, ingredients and nutrition information

- Use a minimum type size or above and high colour contrast, preferably black on white

- Provide clearer and more consistent information about allergens, including plain English to describe ingredients.

*Food labelling requirements in the USA*

Although drafted somewhat differently to legislation in the EU, US food labelling regulations put broadly similar constraints on the food packaging industry in terms of what can be labelled and how it must be displayed. In many cases the US legislation is more prescriptive. Some of the main points that impinge on packaging design and construction are outlined below.

US legislation introduces the concept of the principal display panel (PDP), which is that portion of the package label that is most likely to be seen by the consumer at the time of purchase (there may be more than one PDP on a package). Either all or certain specified label statements must be placed on the PDP. In the latter case, other labelling information is placed on the information panel (the label panel immediately to the right of the PDP as seen by the consumer facing the product - if this panel is not usable, due to package design and construction, (e.g., folded flaps), then the information panel is the next label panel immediately to the right.).

The statement of identity, or name of the food, and the net quantity statement, or amount of product, must appear on the PDP.

The phrase "information panel labelling" refers to the label statements that are generally required to be placed together, without any intervening material, on the information panel, if such labelling does not appear on the PDP. These label statements include the name and address of the manufacturer, packer or distributor, the ingredient list, and nutrition labelling.

For information panel labelling, a prominent print or type size must be used that is conspicuous and easy to read. Letters must be at least one-sixteenth of an inch in height based on the lower case letter "o", and must not be more than three times as high as they are wide; the lettering must also contrast sufficiently with the background so as to be easy to read. Smaller type sizes may be used for information panel labelling on very small food packages

Non-essential, intervening material is not permitted to be placed between the required labelling on the information panel (e.g., the bar code is not required labelling).

Food labels must list:

a.  The name and address of the manufacturer, packer or distributor. Unless the name given is the actual manufacturer, it must be accompanied by a qualifying phrase which states the firm's relation to the product, e.g., "manufactured for" or "distributed by."

b.  The street address, if the firm's name and address are not listed in a current city directory or telephone book; and other address details (e.g. city, state and zip code).

In contrast to the situation in the EU, food nutrition labelling is required for most prepared foods in the US. The required information is also a little more extensive and includes a statement of percentage of the recommended daily allowance that a portion of the food contains. Nutrition labelling for raw produce (fruits and vegetables) and fish is voluntary. Other exemptions exist for food produced by small businesses, and for food which is being given away. Also individual packages in multi-pack items need not be so labelled if the outer wrap contains all of the required information.

The nutrition information must appear in a panel headed 'Nutrition Facts', either on the PDP or on the Information Panel (except for small packages). There are also prescribed ways in which this panel must be displayed, and for the type size used.

When a package contains two or more packaged foods that are intended to be eaten individually, such as a variety pack of breakfast cereals or when packages may be used interchangeably for the same type of food, such as round ice cream containers, the manufacturer may choose to include separate "Nutrition Facts" panels for each food product, or may use an aggregate "Nutrition Facts" panel.

Full details of the labelling requirements are presented on the US Food and Drug Administration's Center for Food safety and Applied Nutrition website (http://vm.cfsan.fda.gov/~dms/flg-toc.html).

# 4. MAKING PACKAGING COMPATIBLE WITH FOOD TYPE AND PROCESS

When designing a new food product or process, or looking at changes in packaging materials for existing products and processes, it is the overall nature of the final output that must be considered. Rather like composers of words and music, there is no rule for which should be considered first, or whether they always have to be considered together, but the interaction between the two must be considered before either component can be finalised. The variety of combination of needs for different products is vast - small changes in the formulation or use of a food may require a complete change in the packaging material used. Seemingly small variations in packaging materials or design may completely change the shelf-life or use of a food. This section will look at specific examples of food products and processes and discuss, in general terms, why the chosen packaging is used; in some cases there may be more than one suitable type of packaging.

## Breakfast cereals

For packaging for corn flakes and similar products, there are two important specific requirements for the product: prevention of physical damage (i.e. stopping the cereal from being crushed and turning to crumb and powder), and prevention of moisture ingress, so that the product does not become soggy. For the latter requirement, some sort of reclosure system might be an advantage. Cereals tend to be sold in relatively large quantities, so the weight of the packaging is also important.

Plastic boxes with recloseable lids are widely used in both domestic and catering/hotel situations for decanting cereal. These are typically made of polypropylene. However, to use this type of package for individual retail display would be unnecessarily expensive, and would add unwanted weight to the package. It would also require paper-based labelling to be incorporated for customer information. For retail situations there is a much more suitable solution: a flexible

## Box 22 - Migration of packaging components into food

There is a general requirement under UK and European Union law that food packaging components must not be transferred into food during its normal shelf-life to the detriment of the food (i.e. to pose a health risk, or to adversely affect the quality of the food - its flavour, texture or appearance). In the UK, this requirement is covered by the general Materials and Articles in Contact with Food Regulations 1987 (as amended). This legislation also lays down specific requirements for PVC packaging. Any food packaging material completely or partially made with PVC must not contain vinyl chloride monomer in excess of 1mg/kg; in addition, transfer of the monomer to food must not exceed 0.01mg/kg of food. There are also detailed requirements for the substances that can be used in the manufacture of regenerated cellulose film, and for limits on the transfer of some of these substances into food.

The Plastic Materials and Articles in Contact with Food Regulations 1998 (as amended) build on the general regulations and set out specific criteria for all plastic packaging. There is a list of approved monomers and of additives that can be used in food contact plastic materials (this covers all contact with food, not just packaging materials). Specific limits are set for the migration of some of these constituents into food. There are also overall migration limits of 60mg/kg of food for materials used in containers (jars, bottles and the like) with capacities between 500ml and 10L, including stoppers, and $10mg/dm^3$ for other materials. To determine whether a particular plastic formulation meets these criteria, there are four model simulants that are used in laboratory trials to assess the plastic's properties. These are: distilled water; a 3% aqueous solution of acetic acid; 10% ethanol in water solution (or greater, if the alcoholic beverage in question has a higher alcohol content); and rectified olive oil. The regulations specify which simulants should be used for each category of food. In general, there are no simulants listed for dried foods, which are unlikely to take up plastics constituents from contact materials.

bag inside a cardboard carton. The stiff cardboard exterior offers adequate protection against physical damage, and also provides an ideal surface for displaying a large amount of product information, including large pictorial designs and logos, as well as additional information that may be completely unrelated to the product but has good marketing appeal for the target consumer. The contents of cereal packages tend to 'settle' during storage, so a transparent package would probably be a disadvantage. (A warning to this settling effect is often made on the packaging, with the important comment that the product is sold by weight, not volume, and the customer is not being under-sold).

The moisture barrier is provided by the interior bag. This needs to be thick enough and tough enough so that it is not likely to be punctured by the product from the inside during repeated use. However, there is no need for complete transparency in the material, nor for an oxygen barrier (cereals are low-fat products and are not prone to rancidity). The flexibility of the inner bag means that it can be rolled up after opening or clipped with a plastic closure device to largely maintain the moisture barrier. Polyethylene is now widely used, although paper-based inner bags used to dominate, and are still used in some situations. Paper itself does not have moisture barrier properties, but it can be treated waxes to be effective.

### Jam jars

Jam is brightly coloured and generally an aesthetically pleasing product to look at, so a primary advantage of packaging for retail purposes is transparency. Also, as it is not completely solid, a rigid package is required. This must not adversely transfer its constituents to the jam and must be suitable for what is essentially a wet product, i.e. it must not absorb water. The packaging needs to be able to withstand hot filling, to have a wide, recloseable opening, and be resistant to the implements (e.g. knives) used to remove the jam. Glass has been the traditional packaging for jam for centuries. Although relatively heavy, this is not too much of a drawback as jam is sold in quite small quantities. Also, although traditionally a long-life product, capable of being stored at ambient temperatures for many months even when opened, modern formulations with reduced sugar levels and without added artificial preservatives rely on refrigerated storage after opening for preservation. This puts obvious limits on the size of individual jars.

Recently, plastics such as PET have been used for packaging jam and similar products. Their obvious advantage over glass is that they are not prone to breakage, and there is the opportunity to make the container lighter than a glass equivalent. However, the plastic used has to fulfil several of the functions performed by glass. Firstly, it has to be resistant to temperatures around 100°C; jam is hot-filled into containers as part of the preservation process (in effect, the hot filling process kills any microorganisms present in the container that might grow in the product - inverting the jar, so that hot product is in contact with the lid, completes the process). It must not transfer its constituents to the jam: the fact that jam is a wet and slightly acid product might make monomer transfer a potential issue. It is also preferable that it be as rigid and clear as glass, and as scratch-resistant. The consumer has become used to the aesthetic properties of glass and will expect an alternative to match these as well as have the extra benefits that plastics can bring.

**Soft drinks bottles**

Soft drinks are another group of product that for decades were traditionally dispensed in glass bottles. Soft drinks are particularly susceptible to tainting, and so an inert, impermeable container is required. For concentrated cordials, the bottle needs to be designed so that small quantities of liquid can easily be poured out and the bottle reclosed. For carbonated beverages, it also needs to have good gas barrier properties, to prevent excess loss of the carbon dioxide during storage.

Since the late 1960s, various plastics solutions have been tried in many traditional glass areas, but bottles have been a primary target. Acrylonitrile polymers were an early proposed solution, but concerns over excessive migration of constituents into the food or drink meant that they were short-lived. The success of PVC has been limited by concerns over environmental issues. It was not until the early 1980s that PET bottles were first introduced commercially, by the Coca-Cola Company (Braakman, 2002). The advent of PET bottles meant that the weight of the packaging could be reduced (with advantages to the consumer and to the manufacturer in reduced transport costs) and the significant risk of glass breakage was eliminated. The lighter weight of the plastic (partially due to the fact that the plastic does not need to made as thick as the glass alternative) has resulted in large-volume containers becoming much more commonplace. Coca-Cola used this to great effect when introducing PET bottles; in a stagnating market, they replaced their one-litre glass bottles with 1-5-litre PET bottles, with no increase in weight. The result was an immediate 27% increase in sales (Braakman, 2002). The development of this trend to larger bottle sizes has, in some cases, necessitated the provision of handles as part of the bottle, something that was not technically feasible with glass. Although it does not have excellent gas barrier properties (it is especially permeable to oxygen), the barrier level to carbon dioxide with the thickness used is suitable for the retention of carbonation in these products.

Another important consideration in the change from glass to plastic bottles for such a large and wide-ranging market as soft drinks was that product processing and filling lines only needed minor readjustments. This was especially relevant for the many small producers in this area.

### 'Canned' foods

The canning operation was developed as a method for taking very perishable raw ingredients (fruit, vegetables, fish and meat) and preserving them principally by heating. At the time it was first introduced, metal and glass containers were the only suitable materials to use. Although the initial experiments were carried out with glass, metal containers quickly became the norm, because of ease of production, their non-breakable nature and weight constraints, among other issues. The fact that we are now 200 years on from the first developments and this type of product still forms a major food category, which remains dominated by metal containers, is testament to the value of the original concept. What does this type of product require? As the process involves high temperatures and both steam and water, a non-corroding material is essential. It must also be able to be hermetically sealed, but it does not need to be resealable: once the hermetic seal is broken, the unique quality of the product (i.e. its sterility) will be lost. Cans and their contents have largely been designed to be used in one go. Canned food is not often brightly coloured and so transparency of material is not an issue. Steel (and latterly aluminium) cans fulfil these basic requirements cost-effectively.

The wide variation in types of products that are processed in this way has meant that many variations in container properties have arisen. Metals are generally fairly chemically reactive, especially in the presence of oxygen. It is highly desirable to have as small a headspace as possible in a hermetically sealed metal can (i.e. the can should be as full as product as possible). This reduces the amount of oxygen that might be present to a minimum. The effect of oxygen, especially in unlacquered cans, is clearly seen if an opened can, perhaps half-filled with product, is left out for any length of time; the inside of the can quickly becomes oxidised and tarnished. Although not necessarily a major health hazard, if this type of reaction occurred in the unopened can (unless significant tin levels accumulated), tainting and chemical deterioration of the product would be a major concern. Therefore, canned foods in metal containers come with the general warning that they should not be left opened for any significant length of time. As well as a direct effect on the metal of the container, oxygen can promote or accelerate interactions between the food itself and the container. Thus, problems, if they occur, are often greatest at the food/headspace interface.

Canned foods such as fruits and rhubarb are quite acidic, and will react with the metal container quite readily. Meat and fish products, with a high sulphur content, may also react with the metal, resulting in blackening or sulphide staining of the container. Quality of product and shelf-life may be enhanced in these products by using lacquered containers. The type of lacquer used will depend on the type of food in the can and also to an extent on the visual effect that is desired: recently, titanium dioxide-pigmented lacquers have been used in tomato-based canned foods to give a 'clean' look to the can, and also to show off the red colour of the tomato.

There has recently been a resurgence in the use of glass for the packaging of in-container sterilized food. The main objections to the use of glass are its extra cost and its fragility. Canned foods are usually high-volume, low-cost foods. In supermarkets, the display for sale of these commodities usually involves stacking of cans in several layers - this would clearly be a problem if the product were packed in glass. Although glass has one major advantage over metal - its inertness to the product - this is not usually enough to outweigh the disadvantages. However, for higher-cost, lower-volume products, especially those that can benefit from the transparency of glass, it does become a viable option. Foods packed in this way include brightly coloured fruits and vegetables.

Most recently, plastics have been used for this type of product. The plastics have to be able to withstand sterilisation times and temperatures (e.g. 30 minutes at 121°C), have seals that will not leak, not be significantly permeable to oxygen over extended storage times (e.g. several years) and not transfer their constituents to the food. Finding a single plastic that fulfils all of these functions adequately is a tall order and multi-layer laminates were developed to solve problem. The question of rigidity also has to be considered. Is the product suitable for presenting in a completely flexible pouch, or does it need to be in a rigid or semi-rigid container?

Flexible containers were first produced as triple laminates, consisting of polyester, aluminium foil and polypropylene. The polyester exterior is used for high-temperature resistance, toughness and the ability to print on label details. The label can be reverse printed (i.e. the ink is embedded between the polyester and the aluminium foil) or conventionally printed. The aluminium foil layer is normally laminated with the matt finish exposed to view. It provides a good barrier to both light and gases for extended shelf life. The polypropylene provides the critical heat-seal integrity, flexibility and strength characteristics. It is also compatible from a taste and odour point of view with a variety of food products (Downing, 1996). Although this laminate combination has proved quite successful, after this type of pouch was first introduced, problems were noted with the occasional formation of pinhole perforations in the fabric of the pouch, which negated the sterility of the product. As well as the possibility of product leakage, this poses a real threat of product spoilage in some way, and the likelihood of pathogenic microorganisms gaining entry to the food. In more recent laminate pouch packages, an extra layer of nylon has been incorporated to provide much more resistance to tearing and the formation of pinhole perforations. Generally, any type of sterilized product that can be packaged in metal cans or glass can now be packaged in flexible containers. Given that similar product qualities can be achieved in each of these types of package, the choice of which to use will largely depend on the convenience of the packaging itself: for example, metals cans for ease of stacking and resistance to rough treatment in warehouses, etc., glass for 'showing off' the product, and flexible pouches for lightweight nature and the ability to be easily transported by the consumer - carrying around flexible pouches in a rucksack, for example, is considerably easier than carrying around metal cans.

Plastics are also now used for semi-rigid retortable containers such as plastic pots with foil lids. The basic structure of the rigid pot is two layers of polypropylene with a sandwich filling of polyvinylidene chloride or ethylene vinyl alcohol polymer as a gas barrier. In addition to the usual barrier properties, the lids for these containers must be able to be easily sealed to the container and must be easy to open. As with flexible pouches, the exterior surface is polyester for printability, and scuff and tear resistance; relatively thick aluminium foil is used for stiffness and to provide a light, moisture and oxygen barrier, and the interior heat seal component comprises polypropylene film.

## Aseptic processing

In aseptic packaging, the food and package are sterilised separately, and then the product is filled into the container under aseptic conditions before the container is sealed. It has the advantage over conventional canning in that it is potentially easier to control the product sterilisation process and prevent 'over-cooking' of product, so enabling a better quality product to be produced. This is particularly true for liquid (e.g. fruit juice) and semi-liquid products (e.g. custard). Unlike conventional canning operations, there is scope to sterilize the packaging in different ways: in addition to wet or dry heat, ultraviolet light and chemicals such as hydrogen peroxide can be used, either alone, or in combination with each other or with heat. Gamma radiation is also technically efficient.

Generally, however, the package must fulfil the same functions as in canning. It must be capable of withstanding decontamination (e.g. sterilization) conditions, not transfer constituents to the food in any deleterious way, form a barrier to gases such as oxygen, and be resistant to external forces that might break the hermetic seal or in some other way damage the packaging. In addition, the package has to be capable of being easily filled during the processing operation, and it has to be possible to reliably seal the package after filling. Glass jars and metal containers can be used for such operations, but plastics and plastic films, paper, and metal foils and sheets are the commonly used materials. As with retortable plastic packages, there is currently no single plastic material that, by itself, has all of the characteristics that are desirable or necessary for packages for aseptically processed foods (Downing, 1996), and so laminations of two or more plastics with different properties, with or without other layers, are used.

## Box 23 - Aseptic packaging of fruit juices

Fruit juices provide a good example of how the nature of a product and the way in which it is used by the consumer can influence the way it is processed and packaged. Aseptic processing offers an excellent method of producing long-life (sterilised) fruit juice of good organoleptic and nutritional quality (being able to optimise and minimise the sterilisation process allows for good retention of vitamin C, for example). Fruit juices tend to be consumed in small, but regular quantities; the most economical way of providing the product to the consumer is in a relatively large volume, designed to provide several servings over a fairly short space of time (one only has to compare the price, say, of a 1-litre carton of orange juice with a small, single-portion sachet to demonstrate this). Being a liquid, the packaging needs to be able to be stood upright after opening. Metal in contact with fruit juice after opening could result in rapid oxidation reactions, with tainting concomitantly occurring; traditional metal can-type packages are also not easy to re-seal. Glass jars can be used and are easy to reseal, but are relatively expensive for what has become a high-volume, low-cost product. The solution offered by systems such as the Tetra-Pak system has addressed the needs very effectively. This consists of multiple layers of plastics, paper and aluminium foil. The Tetra-Pak and Pure-Pak packaging consists of a polyethylene exterior and interior, sandwiching layers of paperboard (on which is printed label information), polyethylene, aluminium foil and surlyn (an ethylene/methacrylic acid copolymer developed by Du Pont) (Du Pont, 2003). This combination yields a semi-rigid packaging that can stand upright after opening.

More recently, various types of closure systems have been developed for this type of package. Fruit juice pulp will settle out of the juice fraction quite quickly, and the ability to 'shake before use' is a distinct advantage. Vitamin C, one of the more important nutritional components in fruit juice, is readily oxidised in air, and even a relatively unsophisticated closure will help limit the loss of the vitamin during storage after opening.

**Fresh meat and fish**

The use of packaging for fresh products like meat and fish is a relatively new development, but it does offer significant improvements in quality and convenience as well as shelf-life extension.

Joints of meat are often tightly wrapped in plastic. This excludes air and so can significantly reduce the rate of development of oxidative rancidity, as well as preventing drying out or physical contamination. In combination with chilled storage, it can also reduce the rate of growth of spoilage microorganisms. However, care has to be taken not to introduce the risk of growth of the pathogen, *Clostridium botulinum,* and the shelf-life of such products is limited to a maximum of a few days.

Cuts of meat and fillets of fish are now frequently displayed in film-sealed trays. The trays need to be rigid enough to hold the food and be able to be effectively sealed to the lidding film. Expanded polystyrene is extremely lightweight and is an ideal material. Fresh meat and fish tend to drip blood or water in significant amounts, which would quickly make the product look unsightly, and limit its shelf-life. This can be off-set by the incorporation of water-absorbing materials into the tray. These usually consist of a highly absorbent material such as polyacrylate, sandwiched between a material that is suitable for food contact, such as polypropylene or polyethylene (see section 5.2 on active packaging). The package itself may well be gas flushed - i.e. the air in it is replaced with an artificial gas mixture (see section 5.1 on modified atmosphere packaging). The use of a high-oxygen gas mixture can help preserve the redness of fresh meat. If the product has been packaged under a modified atmosphere, it is important that the lidding film is effectively sealed to the tray, and that it is impermeable to the gases used. Lidding films typically used are combinations of LDPE and PVdC with either PET or polyamide, or PC/EVOH/EVA (Air Products, 1995). In these situations, a clear film is desired to show off the contents to best effect.

In addition to the packaging that will keep the product in the best possible condition, the package also needs to contain labelling information. By far the simplest means of doing this is to create an outer card sleeve that slips over the package. This allows a wide range of label formats and designs to be used, with the customer still able to see the food within the package.

Chilled and frozen ready meals, which have enjoyed great market success over the past 25-30 years, use many of the packaging techniques described here. However, their packaging will also depend on how the product is to be reheated or cooked (see below), as the material used may have to be able to withstand temperatures of 200°C and above.

## Fresh fruits and vegetables

As with fish and meat, the packaging of fruits and vegetables is a relatively new development, and it brings with it one phenomenon that makes them significantly different to all other food types. Whether the fruit or vegetables are whole or put/peeled/trimmed etc., they will continue to respire after they have been packed, using up oxygen and producing carbon dioxide and water. Packaging therefore has to take this into account. When 'bagging up' whole fruit and vegetables, small holes are usually left in the package to prevent excessive condensation.

The packaging of cut, prepared fruit and vegetables in some sort of controlled or modified atmosphere, to prevent rapid over-ripening and/or spoilage, is now quite well developed. [The techniques of modified atmosphere packaging (MAP), in which a gas mixture other than air is incorporated into the pack, and active packaging (which can be used to control the gas atmosphere in the pack) are described in later sections.] Without specialised packaging, this type of product would have a shelf-life of hours; controlling or modifying the atmosphere in the pack can allow this to be extended to several days. Polystyrene trays are again suitable containers, but the lidding film usually has some degree of gas permeability, so that excessive oxygen depletion and carbon dioxide build up do not occur. There are two broad techniques to achieve this. In passive controlled atmosphere packaging, the size of the pack and the type of film are chosen so that the desired atmosphere is reached as a result of produce respiration. In active controlled atmosphere packaging the desired gas composition is applied, and the porosity of the packaging film is adjusted so that this composition is maintained. Moisture production and loss also have to be balanced.

## Microwave-reheatable ready meals

In designing foods suitable for cooking or reheating in the packaging, either using microwave cooking or traditional ovens or both, special care has to be taken to ensure that the packaging is also suitable for the purpose.

The nature of microwave heating is radically different from that of a conventional oven. In a conventional oven, heat from the surroundings migrates into the product in a more-or-less even fashion, giving a fairly uniform temperature gradient from the outside to the cooler interior. Eventually, the product would reach temperature equilibrium, but no part would be hotter than the oven. In a microwave, radiation energy penetrates into the food and causes a heating effect. Although the amount of radiation contacting the food components is greatest at the surface, different components will absorb more energy and heat up more quickly than others. Therefore, hot and cold spots can easily be formed, and the surface is not always the hottest part. Also, the hot areas will continue to absorb energy, and so there is no upper limit to how hot the product can become (while the oven temperature stays relatively unchanged). As well as a potential safety issue, the formation of hotspots is of significance in product quality issues and for packaging (if serious, the food can melt the packaging). The different rates that individual components will heat up at in a multi-component food is especially an issue with frozen food, as once a component melts, it will absorb microwave energy much more quickly than one that is still frozen, so that some parts may become very hot before another has defrosted. Research at CCFRA (Burnett and George, 1993) demonstrated that, in some cases, one component had become charred before another had defrosted. This means not only that the packaging must give the consumer adequate reheating instructions, but also that the physical location of the food within the package must be considered. In some cases it may require modification of the package shape.

Before the advent of microwave reheating, aluminium trays dominated the market for reheatable ready meals and similar concepts. The trays, being non-tainting and simple in design (rectangular base with sloping sides of variable height) are easy and relatively cheap to produce. The tops can be 'crimped' to allow a lid to be physically held in position (as is commonly used in take-away food containers). However, aluminium is not ideal for microwave applications. In early microwave oven designs, arcing occurred when metal objects were placed inside the oven, as the energy was reflected back into the magnetron. Although modification of oven design has largely removed this risk, there is still customer reticence to use them, and there is evidence to indicate that arcing can still occasionally occur. In addition, aluminium also acts as a shield to microwave energy. Therefore, food heats significantly more slowly in aluminium-containing packages (Huss, 1997). If metal is used in a microwave, it is essential that there is no metal-to-metal contact, and if it is a metal tray that is being used, it needs to be shallow. This is because of the shielding effect of the base of the tray (i.e. the microwave energy can only heat the food from the top). Aluminium trays have been designed with a plastic base, but these have not been commercialised.

Various plastics formulations now dominate the market for microwave-reheatable food packaging. Obviously, they have to retain sufficient rigidity at elevated temperatures, and must not taint or otherwise adversely affect the product at these temperatures. In most cases the tray section will be sealed with a lidding film, which may or may not be removed before the food is reheated.

High-density polyethylene (HDPE) can be used in some microwave applications, but it starts to lose its rigidity above 95°C, so is only suitable for homogeneous foods with a short heating cycle. Polypropylene is suitable for microwave applications, and was successfully used in the USA in combination with ethyl vinyl alcohol (EVOH) (to improve oxygen barrier properties) for shelf-stable (i.e. non-chilled) meals. Its melting point means that it is not generally suitable for conventional ovens.

Although many other plastics are suitable to some degree for both microwaveable and traditional ovens, polycarbonate and nylon 6/6, amongst others, because of cost, production and adaptability considerations, it is crystallised polyethylene terephthalate (CPET) that has the most widespread applications. It has a higher melting point than polypropylene, and so is less prone to damage by overheating in hotspots.

## Box 24 - Susceptor boards

Because the heat in microwave heating is generated within the product, and the oven air temperature itself is usually only a few degrees above ambient, there is no heating or drying effect at the surface. In general, however, the outer portion of the food will be hotter than the inner, and there will be a net migration of moisture to the surface. The result tends to be a rather soggy surface, which in some products (e.g. pie toppings and pizza bases) is highly undesirable. Susceptor boards are a packaging innovation designed to give a crisping or browning effect to the cooked or reheated product. They consist of card with an immeasurably fine metal layer sprayed onto them. This layer absorbs microwave energy and becomes hot. The heat is then 'used' to dry out the surface of the food and create the browning/crisping effect. As the metal layer is so thin, the amount of heat contained in the layer is quite low (although the temperature might be very high). Therefore, in order to be effective the susceptor must be in close contact with the surface of the food (within 0.2mm). For the same reason, susceptors only work with relatively dry foods - not enough energy can be generated in the board to evaporate water from wet foods.

# 5. SPECIFIC PACKAGING INNOVATIONS

## 5.1 Modified atmosphere packaging

Modified atmosphere packaging (MAP) involves replacing the air in a food package with an artificial gas mixture, in order to prolong the shelf life of the food and improve its sensory characteristics. This, in turn, is likely to increase the availability of the product and reduce wastage (e.g. product exceeding its shelf-life and having to be discarded). Reformulation of the product, e.g. with reduced use of other artificial preservatives, is also feasible in some cases, which might improve the appeal of the product.

Unlike some other novel packaging developments, this technique has become highly developed and widely used throughout the food industry, thanks to the wide variety of plastic packaging materials that have become available for food use. The processing machinery and technology associated with MAP means that the packages are typically flexible or semi-rigid.

In most situations, MAP is used to retard microbial growth, and is usually used in combination with chilled storage to effect this. However, the technique can also be applied to other situations, such as preventing chemical changes in food - principally oxidation. For example, ambient-stable bakery products and snack products such as poppadoms or crisps can be packed in a modified atmosphere (excluding oxygen) to prevent rancidity through fat oxidation. Ensuring that the gas in the package is dry may also slow down the loss of crispness in this type of product.

The nature of the gas mixture will depend on the characteristics of the food being packed. As each gas will interact with different foods in different ways, levels and combinations have to be carefully calculated. The three gases that make up the vast majority of modified atmosphere mixtures are nitrogen, carbon dioxide and oxygen. Other gases, notably argon, have also been investigated, but their use is not as widespread.

### Table 3 - Typical gas mixtures used in MAP of retail products
#### (from Air Products, 1995)

|                                                        | $O_2$ | $CO_2$ | $N_2$ |
|--------------------------------------------------------|-------|--------|-------|
| Raw red meat                                           | 70%   | 30%    |       |
| Raw offal                                              | 80%   | 20%    |       |
| Raw, white fish and other seafood                      | 30%   | 40%    | 30%   |
| Raw poultry and game                                   |       | 30%    | 70%   |
| Cooked, cured and processed meat products              |       | 30%    | 70%   |
| Cooked, cured and processed fish and seafood products  |       | 30%    | 70%   |
| Cooked, cured and processed poultry products           |       | 30%    | 70%   |
| Ready meals and other cook-chill products              |       | 30%    | 70%   |
| Fresh pasta products                                   |       | 50%    | 50%   |
| Bakery products                                        |       | 50%    | 50%   |
| Dairy products                                         |       | 100%   |       |
| Dried foods                                            |       |        | 100%  |
| Liquid foods and drinks                                |       |        | 100%  |

*Characteristics of gases used in MAP*

Carbon dioxide has bacteriostatic and fungistatic properties and retards the growth of most moulds and aerobic bacteria, making it useful in the MAP of moist foods. However, some micro-organisms are not inhibited: lactic acid bacteria grow better in the presence of carbon dioxide, combined with low oxygen levels. Yeasts are also less susceptible to carbon dioxide than moulds and aerobic bacteria.

The inhibitory effect of carbon dioxide is increased at lower temperatures (in addition to the beneficial effect of the lower temperature *per se*). This is because of its enhanced solubility in water (present in the food) to form carbonic acid, which has antimicrobial properties.

There are several factors which can limit the usefulness of carbon dioxide in MAP. The absorption of carbon dioxide into the food is highly dependent on the water and fat content of the food. Excess absorption may cause the package to collapse, through the creation of a partial vacuum. The water-holding capacity of meat and seafood products may be reduced, resulting in an unsightly drip, and some products, such as dairy foods, may be tainted. On a more general note, fresh fruit and vegetables, which continue to respire after packaging, may suffer physiological damage in the presence of elevated carbon dioxide levels (Day, 1992).

In most MAP applications, oxygen levels are kept as low as possible, in order to inhibit the growth of aerobic pathogens and spoilage organisms, and to reduce the rate of oxidative deterioration of foods. However, there are exceptions: oxygen is needed for fruit and vegetable respiration, and for colour retention in red meats. Residual levels of oxygen will also prevent the growth of anaerobic pathogens such as *Clostridium botulinum.* (However, the food packager has to aware of the danger of other (aerobic) organisms using up the remaining oxygen, and thus creating conditions suitable for the anaerobes.) The biochemical and antimicrobial effects of high levels of oxygen have also been researched recently (see box 26).

Nitrogen is effectively inert and has a low solubility in both water and fat. In MAP, nitrogen is used primarily to displace oxygen in order to retard aerobic spoilage and oxidative deterioration. It also acts as a filler gas to prevent pack collapse.

The choice of the gas combination to be used will depend on the nature of the food, and of the micro-organisms associated with that food which will limit the shelf-life. It is also important to bear in mind that preventing the growth of one type of microorganism may allow another group to proliferate. The most notable example of this is in the creation of anaerobic environments, which may allow the growth of *Clostridium botulinum,* an organism that can only grow in the absence of oxygen, and which produces a highly potent neurotoxin when it does grow.

## Box 25 - Other MAP gases

Other gases used experimentally and in limited commercial situations include carbon monoxide, ozone, ethylene oxide, nitrous oxide, helium, neon, argon, propylene oxide, ethanol vapour, hydrogen, sulphur dioxide and chlorine. Several of these have serious health or safety concerns associated with them. For example, carbon monoxide has been shown to be very effective at maintaining the colour of red meats and inhibiting the decay of plant tissue, but it is toxic and is not a permitted packaging gas in the European Union. However, it has been used commercially in Norway for fresh meats (Brydon, 2002).

Argon, which is chemically inert like nitrogen, may have wider applicability. Its atomic size is similar to molecular size of gaseous oxygen and it is denser and more soluble in water than either nitrogen or oxygen. It may thus have biochemical activity, being more effective at displacing molecular oxygen from cellular sites and enzyme receptors, consequently slowing down oxidative deterioration reactions. There are over 200 products packed using argon in the UK, including nuts, crisps, pizzas, meats and drinks (Brydon, 2002).

Both argon and nitrous oxide, which are permitted for use as packaging gases in the European Union, are also thought to sensitise micro-organisms to antimicrobial agents. This may be mediated through alteration of the fluidity of microbial cell walls. A French company, Air Liquide, has filed a number of patents concerning the activity of in MAP of argon and nitrous oxide. One patent claims that both are capable of extending shelf-life by inhibiting fungal growth, reducing ethylene emissions in fresh produce, and slowing down sensory quality deterioration.

### Further reading:

Brydon, L. (2002). Developments in MAP and active packaging. Proceedings of Minimal Processing Conference, Sardinia.

Day, B.P.F. (2001) Fresh prepared produce: GMP for high oxygen MAP and non-sulphite dipping. Guideline No. 31. Campden & Chorleywood Food Research Association

Fath, D. and Soudain, P. (1992) Method for the preservation of fresh vegetables. US Patent No. 5,128,160

## Box 26 - High-oxygen MAP

Recently there has been much research into the use of high-oxygen MAP for shelf-life extension of fresh prepared products (e.g. chopped fruits and vegetables) and combination products such as sandwiches, pizzas and chilled stir-fry ready meals. The initial thrust was in the prolonged preservation of items that were still respiring and therefore consuming oxygen and producing carbon dioxide and water. These present a special problem to the packager, as the relative changes in gas and moisture content will affect respiration rate and ultimately the quality of the food in quite a complex manner. One way of circumventing this is by using packaging material with specific permeability characteristics, depending on how rapidly the items are respiring - controlled atmosphere packaging. High-oxygen MAP (i.e. 70-100% oxygen) uses a different approach. The high level of oxygen delays the problem of oxygen depletion and subsequent growth of anaerobic micro-organisms. It was also found to inhibit aerobic micro-organisms, which are adapted to oxygen levels of around 21% (i.e. atmospheric levels). It is hypothesised that reactive oxygen species damage vital cellular macromolecules and thereby inhibit microbial growth when oxidative stresses overwhelm cellular antioxidant protection systems.

Biochemical deterioration also appears to be inhibited. The main problem with cut fruits and vegetables is discoloration, caused by oxidation of natural phenolic constituents to colourless quinones, which subsequently polymerise to coloured melanins. This is initiated by the action of the enzyme polyphenol oxidase, and it seems as if high levels of oxygen directly or indirectly inhibit the activity of the enzyme.

Research was subsequently carried out to evaluate the effect of high-oxygen MAP on the shelf-life of stir-fry ready meals, pizzas and sandwiches, all of which have both respiring and non-respiring components. High-oxygen MAP was found to be more effective than nitrogen/carbon dioxide MAP for extending the shelf-life of both pizzas and ready meals, but no such benefit was found with sandwiches, where the critical factors determining shelf-life (bread staling and moisture migration), are not affected by MAP.

### Further reading:

Day, B.P.F. (2001a) Fresh prepared produce: GMP for high oxygen MAP and non-sulphite dipping. Guideline No. 31. Campden & Chorleywood Food Research Association

Day, B.P.F. (2001b) Novel high oxygen MAP for chilled combination food products. R&D Report No. 125. Campden & Chorleywood Food Research Association

*MAP materials*

The choice of gas mixture can not be made in isolation from the choice of packaging material, which in turn is limited by the need to be able to introduce the gas mixture and effectively seal the pack. The following table summarises some of the requirements that the packaging may have to fulfil. These will vary from one product to another.

## Table 4 - Main requirements of an MA package

- *Contain the product and gas (seal integrity)*
- *Be compatible with the food*
- *Be non-toxic*
- *Withstand the packaging process*
- *Handle distribution stresses*
- *Prevent physical damage*
- *Possess appropriate gas permeability*
- *Control moisture loss or gain*
- *Possess antifog properties and be transparent*
- *Prevent microbial, chemical and physical contamination*
- *Be easy to open*
- *Be tolerant to operational temperatures (e.g. microwave cooking)*

Gas permeability of the packaging material is one of the principal considerations in MAP. In most cases, it is desirable to maintain the applied gas mixture for as long as possible. Therefore, the packaging material should have barrier properties. The permeability of a particular packaging material depends on several factors, such as the nature of the gas, the structure and thickness of the material, the temperature and the relative humidity. Materials are generally 3-5 times more permeable to carbon dioxide than to oxygen, and 3-5 times more permeable to oxygen than to nitrogen. Some materials, such as nylon and ethylene-vinyl alcohol are moisture sensitive and their gas permeabilities depend on the relative humidity. Generally, materials with an oxygen permeability of less than 50 $cm^3/m^2/day/atmosphere$ are used. For respiring produce (i.e. fresh prepared fruits and vegetables), it is usually desirable to have materials with enhanced gas permeability, so that the atmosphere can be controlled over a period of time.

As well as gas barrier properties, the packaging materials need to have water vapour barrier properties that prevent undesirable moisture loss from the product. These vary considerably from one material to another, and are not related to the materials' gas permeabilities.

Materials used must have sufficient strength to resist puncture, withstand repeated flexing and endure the mechanical stresses encountered during handling. Poor mechanical properties can lead to pack damage and gas leakage. As part of this, it is essential that the package can be effectively sealed. However, it will also need to be easily opened by the consumer, which requires a specific balance of properties.

Typical MA packages consist of semi-rigid trays with heat-sealed foil lids, pillow packs (such as those used for packaging chocolate bars) and bulk bag-in-box and master pack containers (e.g. the food is contained within a modified atmosphere flexible package, which itself is enclosed within a more rigid box).

*Introducing the gas*

There are three techniques to replace the air within MA packages: gas flushing, compensated vacuum and passive modification.

In gas flushing, the replacement of air inside the package is performed by a continuous gas stream, which dilutes the air surrounding the food product before the package is sealed. The great advantage of this technique is the speed of the machine; since the dilution of air is continuous, the packaging rate can be very high. However, since air replacement is by dilution, there is a limit to the efficiency of the technique, and typical residual oxygen levels achieved are 2-5%. Therefore, for foods that are particularly oxygen sensitive, gas flushing is not normally suitable.

In the compensated vacuum technique, air is removed by pulling a partial vacuum on the air within the package, and then this is broken with the desired gas mixture. As this is a two-step process, it is considerably slower than gas flushing, but it does allow much lower residual oxygen levels to be achieved and so is suitable for foods which are particularly oxygen-sensitive.

Passive modification occurs when respiring fruit and vegetables are enclosed in sealed packages: the oxygen present is used up and converted to carbon dioxide. This is independent of any modified atmosphere that is incorporated by the above methods.

It is also possible to incorporate liquid nitrogen into rigid cans, bottles and jars, to reduce in-pack oxygen levels and pressurise the container. This technique is predominantly applicable to ambient-stable dried products such as nuts, coffee, milk powder and dried potato, and retards deleterious oxidation reactions.

## 5.2 Active packaging

Active packaging refers to the incorporation of certain additives into packaging film or containers with the aim of maintaining and extending product quality and shelf-life. Packaging may be termed active when it performs some desired role in food preservation other than providing an inert barrier to external conditions. The release of tin into canned foods is one form of active packaging system, but the development of a whole range of systems, some of which may have application in both new and existing food products, is fairly new. Active packaging includes additives or "freshness enhancers" that are capable of:

- scavenging oxygen
- adsorbing carbon dioxide, moisture, ethylene and/or flavour/odour taints
- releasing ethanol, sorbates, antioxidants and/or other preservatives
- catalysing the removal of lactose and cholesterol
- maintaining temperature control.

Active packaging has been used with many food products and is being tested with numerous others. The shelf-life of packaged food is dependent on numerous factors such as the intrinsic nature of the food (e.g. pH, water activity, nutrient content, occurrence of antimicrobial compounds, redox potential, respiration rate and biological structure) and extrinsic factors (e.g. storage temperature, relative humidity and the surrounding gaseous composition). These factors will directly influence the chemical, biochemical, physical and microbiological spoilage mechanisms of individual food products and their achievable shelf-lives. Knowledge of these in some cases allows active packaging systems to be developed to prolong shelf-lives. The active packaging device needs to be carefully matched to the food type, package type and headspace size and composition to be effective.

*Oxygen scavengers*

Oxygen scavengers are by far the most commercially important sub-category of active packaging. The global market for oxygen scavengers was estimated to exceed 10 billion units in Japan, several hundred million in the USA and tens of million in Europe in 1996. The value of this market in 1996 was estimated to exceed $200 million (Anon, 1996a; Rooney, 1998). Oxygen can have considerable detrimental effects on foods. Oxygen scavengers can therefore help maintain food product quality by decreasing food metabolism, reducing oxidative rancidity, inhibiting undesirable oxidation of labile pigments and vitamins, controlling enzymic discoloration and inhibiting the growth of aerobic microorganisms.

The most well-known oxygen scavengers take the form of small sachets containing various iron based powders with an assortment of catalysts. These chemical systems often react with water supplied by the food to produce a reactive hydrated metallic reducing agent, which scavenges oxygen within the food package and irreversibly converts it to a stable oxide. The iron powder is separated from the food. often by keeping it in a small, highly oxygen permeable sachet which is labelled 'Do not eat'. The main advantage of using such oxygen scavengers is that they are capable of reducing oxygen levels to less than 0.01%, which is much lower that the typical 0.3-3.0% residual oxygen levels achievable by modified atmosphere packaging (MAP). Oxygen scavengers can be used alone or in combination with MAP. Their use alone eliminates the need for MAP machinery and can increase packaging speeds.

However, it is usually more common commercially to remove most of the atmospheric oxygen by MAP and then use a relatively small and inexpensive scavenger to mop up the residual oxygen remaining within the food package.

Non-metallic oxygen scavengers have also been developed to alleviate the potential for metallic taints being imparted to food products. Non-metallic scavengers include those that use organic reducing agents such as ascorbic acid, ascorbate salts or catechol. They also include enzymic oxygen scavenger systems using either glucose oxidase or ethanol oxidase which could be incorporated into sachets or adhesive labels, or immobilised onto packaging film surfaces (Hurme and Ahveainen, 1996).

Oxygen scavengers were first marketed in Japan in 1976 by the Mitsubishi Gas Chemical Co. Ltd. under the trade name Ageless™ (Day, 1999). Oxygen scavenger technology has been successful in Japan for a variety of reasons including the acceptance by Japanese consumers of innovative packaging and the hot and humid climate in Japan during the summer months which is conducive to mould spoilage of food products, and so makes oxygen scavengers especially beneficial. In contrast to the Japanese market, the acceptance of oxygen scavengers in North America and Europe has been slow, although several manufacturers and distributors of oxygen scavengers are now established in both these continents (Day, 1999).

The potential danger of consumers accidentally eating these scavengers has mainly been circumvented by the development of oxygen-scavenging adhesive labels that can be adhered to the inside of packages and the incorporation of scavengers into laminated trays and plastic films. However, the speed and capacity of oxygen scavenging plastic films and laminated trays are considerably lower than iron-based oxygen scavenger sachets or labels.

Marks & Spencer plc were the first UK retailer to use oxygen scavenging adhesive labels for a range of sliced cooked and cured meat and poultry products which are particularly sensitive to deleterious light and oxygen-induced colour changes. Other UK retailers, distributors and caterers are now using these labels for such food products as well as for coffee, pizzas, speciality bakery goods and dried food ingredients. Other food applications for oxygen scavenger labels and sachets include cakes, breads, biscuits, croissants, fresh pastas, cured fish, tea, powdered milk, dried egg, spices, herbs, confectionery and snack foods (Day, 1999).

The use of oxygen scavengers for beer, wine and other beverages is potentially a huge market. Iron based label and sachet scavengers cannot be used for beverages because their oxygen scavenging capability is rapidly lost when wet. Instead, various non-metallic reagents and organo-metallic compounds which have an affinity for oxygen have been incorporated into bottle closures, crown and caps so that any oxygen present is scavenged from the bottle headspace.

*Moisture absorbers*

Excess moisture is a major cause of food spoilage. Soaking up moisture by using various absorbers or desiccants is very effective at maintaining food quality and extending shelf-life by inhibiting microbial growth and moisture related degradation of texture and flavour. Several companies manufacture moisture absorbers in the form of sachets, pads, sheets or blankets. For packaged dried food applications, desiccants such as silica gel, calcium oxide and activated clays and minerals are typically contained within tear-resistant permeable plastic sachets. For dual-action purposes, these sachets may also contain activated carbon for odour adsorption or iron powder for oxygen scavenging.

The use of moisture absorber sachets is common in Japan where popular foods feature a number of dried products that need to be protected from humidity damage. In the UK, silica gel-based moisture-absorbing sachets have been used for maintaining the crispness of filled ciabatta bread rolls.

In addition to moisture absorber sachets for humidity control in packaged dried foods, several companies manufacture moisture drip absorbent pads, sheets and blankets for liquid water control in high water activity foods such as meats, fish, poultry, fruit and vegetables. Basically they consist of two layers of a microporous non-woven plastic film, such as polyethylene or polypropylene, between which is placed a superabsorbent polymer which is capable of absorbing up to 500 times its own weight of water. Typical superabsorbent polymers include polyacrylate salts and starch copolymers which both have a very strong affinity for water. Moisture drip absorber pads are commonly placed under packaged fresh meats, fish and poultry to absorb unsightly tissue drip exudate. Larger sheets and blankets are used for absorption of melted ice from chilled seafood during air freight transportation or for controlling transpiration of horticultural produce.

Another approach for the control of excess moisture in high water activity foods is to intercept the moisture in the vapour phase. This approach allows food packers or even householders to decrease the water activity on the surface of foods by reducing in-pack relative humidity. This can be done by placing one or more humectants between two layers of water permeable plastic film. For example, the Japanese company Showa Denko Co. Ltd has developed a Pitchit™ film which consists of a layer of humectant carbohydrate and propylene glycol sandwiched between two layers of polyvinyl alcohol (PVA) plastic film. Pitchit™ film is marketed for home use in a roll or single sheet form for wrapping fresh meats, fish and poultry. After wrapping in this film, the surface of the food is dehydrated by osmotic pressure, resulting in microbial inhibition and a reported shelf-life extension of 3-4 days under chilled storage (Day, 1999).

*Carbon dioxide scavengers*

There are many commercial sachet and label devices that can be used to either scavenge or emit carbon dioxide. In different situations, the presence or build-up of carbon dioxide may be beneficial - it is an effective antimicrobial agent; in others it may be a problem - depressing respiration of fresh fruit and vegetables or causing packages to swell or distort.

The use of carbon dioxide scavengers is particularly applicable for fresh roasted or ground coffees, which produce significant volumes of carbon dioxide. Fresh roasted or ground coffees cannot be left unpackaged since they will absorb moisture and oxygen and lose desirable volatile aromas and flavours. However, if coffee is hermetically sealed in packs directly after roasting, the carbon dioxide released will build up within the packs and eventually cause them to burst (Subramanian, 1998).

To circumvent this problem, two solutions are currently used. The first is to use packaging with patented one-way valves that will allow excess carbon dioxide to escape. The second solution is to use a carbon dioxide scavenger or a dual-action oxygen and carbon dioxide scavenger system. A mixture of calcium oxide and activated charcoal has been used in polyethylene coffee pouches to scavenge carbon dioxide but dual-action oxygen and carbon dioxide scavenger sachets and labels are more common and are commercially used for canned and foil pouched coffees in Japan and the USA (Anon, 1998; Rooney, 1995). These dual-action sachets and labels typically contain iron powder for scavenging oxygen, and calcium hydroxide which scavenges carbon dioxide by converting it to calcium carbonate under sufficiently high humidity conditions.

Carbon dioxide emitting sachet and label devices can either be used alone or combined with an oxygen scavenger. Pack collapse or the development of a partial vacuum can be a problem for foods packed with an oxygen scavenger. To overcome this problem, dual-action oxygen scavenger/carbon dioxide emitter sachets and labels have been developed which absorb oxygen and generate an equal volume of carbon dioxide. These sachets and labels usually contain ferrous carbonate and a metal halide catalyst, although non-ferrous variants are available (Day, 1999).

*Ethylene scavengers*

Ethylene is a widely-occurring plant hormone which accelerates the senescence (aging) of horticultural products such as fruit, vegetables and flowers. Many of the effects of ethylene are necessary (e.g. induction of flowering in pineapples and colour development in citrus fruits, bananas and tomatoes) but in most horticultural situations it is desirable to remove ethylene or to suppress its effects (e.g. to slow down the ripening process in fruits such as tomatoes). Consequently, much research effort has been undertaken to incorporate ethylene scavengers into fresh produce packaging and storage areas, but it has only met with limited success (Day, 1999).

Effective systems utilise potassium permanganate immobilised on an inert mineral substrate such as alumina or silica gel. Potassium permanganate oxidises ethylene to acetate and ethanol and in the process changes colour from purple to brown and hence indicates its remaining ethylene scavenging capacity. Ethylene scavengers based on potassium permanganate are available in sachets to be placed inside produce packages or inside blankets or tubes that can be placed in produce storage warehouses. Activated carbon-based scavengers with various metal catalysts can also effectively remove ethylene.  They have been used to scavenge ethylene from produce warehouses or incorporated into sachets for inclusion into produce packs or embedded into paper bags or corrugated board boxes for produce storage.  A dual-action ethylene scavenger and moisture absorber has been marketed in Japan; the sachets contain activated carbon, a metal catalyst and silica gel and are capable of scavenging ethylene as well as acting as a moisture absorber (Day, 1999)

*Ethanol emitters*

The use of ethanol as an antimicrobial agent is well documented.  It is particularly effective against mould but can also inhibit the growth of yeasts and bacteria. Although ethanol can be sprayed directly onto food products just prior to packaging, a more practical and safer method of generating ethanol is through the use of ethanol emitting films and sachets. Many applications of ethanol emitting films and sachets have been patented, primarily by Japanese manufacturers.  Ethanol emitters are used extensively in Japan to extend the mould-free shelf-life of high ratio cakes (those with elevated levels of sugar and liquid, resulting in products with a moister, lighter crumb) and other high moisture bakery products by up to 2000% (Rooney, 1995).

All of these films and sachets contain absorbed or encapsulated ethanol in a carrier material which allows the controlled release of ethanol vapour. Moisture is absorbed by the sachet contents and ethanol vapour is released and diffuses into the package headspace. The size and capacity of the ethanol emitting sachet used depends on the weight of food, the water activity of the food and the desired shelf-life required. For example, Ethicap™, which is the most commercially popular ethanol emitter in Japan, consists of food grade alcohol (55%) and water (10%) adsorbed onto silicon dioxide powder (35%) and contained in a sachet made of a paper and ethyl vinyl acetate (EVA) copolymer laminate.  To mask the odour of alcohol, some sachets contain traces of vanilla or other flavours.  The sachets are labelled "Do not eat contents" and include a diagram illustrating this warning.

Research has also shown that bakery products packed with ethanol emitting sachets do not get as hard as those packed without and results are better than using an oxygen scavenger alone to inhibit mould growth. This suggests that ethanol vapour may also exert an anti-staling effect in addition to its anti-mould properties. Ethanol emitting sachets are also widely used in Japan for extending the shelf-life of semi-moist and dry fish products (Rooney, 1995).

*Preservative releasers*

Recently there has been great interest in the potential use of antimicrobial and antioxidant packaging films which have preservative properties for extending the shelf-life of a wide range of food products. These act either by releasing volatile components into the headspace of the package, or by directly contacting the food. As with other categories of active packaging, many patents exist and some antimicrobial and antioxidant films have been marketed, but the majority have so far failed to be commercialised because of doubts about their effectiveness, economic factors and/or regulatory constraints.

Some commercial antimicrobial films and materials have been introduced, primarily in Japan. For example, one widely reported product is a synthetic silver zeolite, which has been directly incorporated into food contact packaging film. The purpose of the zeolite is apparently to allow slow release of antimicrobial silver ions onto the surface of food products. Many other synthetic and naturally occurring preservatives have been proposed and/or tested for antimicrobial activity in plastic and edible films. These include organic acids (e.g. propionate, benzoate and sorbate), bacteriocins (e.g. nisin), spice and herb extracts (e.g. from rosemary, cloves, horseradish, mustard, cinnamon and thyme), enzymes (e.g. peroxidase, lysozyme and glucose oxidase), chelating agents (e.g. EDTA), inorganic acids (e.g. sulphur dioxide and chlorine dioxide) and anti-fungal agents (e.g. imazalil and benomyl). The major potential food applications for antimicrobial films include meats, fish, bread, cheese, fruit and vegetables (Labuza and Breene, 1989).

*Flavour and odour adsorbers*

The interaction of packaging with food flavours and aromas has long been recognised. The unwanted removal of desirable flavours from products has been demonstrated, such as limonene loss in aseptically packed orange juice after just two weeks (Rooney, 1995).

Commercially, very few active packaging techniques have been used to selectively remove undesirable flavours and taints, but many potential opportunities exist. One example is the debittering of pasteurised orange juices. Some varieties of orange, such as Navel, are particularly prone to bitter flavours caused by limonin, a tetraterpenoid that is liberated into the juice after orange pressing and subsequent pasteurisation. Processes have been developed for debittering such juices by passing them through columns of cellulose triacetate or nylon beads (Rooney, 1995). A possible active packaging solution would be to include limonin adsorbers (e.g. cellulose triacetate or acetylated paper) into orange juice packaging material.

Other examples include materials to adsorb and/or oxidise amines that are formed from the breakdown of fish muscle proteins, and aldehydes, such as hexanal and heptanal (which contribute to rancidity), formed by the auto-oxidation of fats and oils.

*Temperature control packaging*

Temperature control active packaging includes the use of innovative insulating materials and self-heating and self-cooling cans. For example, to guard against undue temperature abuse during storage and distribution of chilled foods, special insulating materials have been developed. One such material is Thinsulate™ (3M Company, USA) which is a special non-woven plastic with many air pore spaces. Another approach for maintaining chilled temperatures is to increase the thermal mass of the food package so that it is capable of withstanding temperature rises.

Self-heating cans and containers have been commercially available for decades and are particularly popular in Japan. Self-heating aluminium and steel cans and containers for sake, coffee, tea and ready meals are heated by an exothermic reaction when lime and water positioned in the base are mixed. Similar systems have recently been trialled in the UK, with the Nescafe coffee 'Hot When You Want' can. Although it won two significant innovation awards in the UK in 2002, Nestle is looking for improvements in the design, including abuse-resistance and some sort of temperature capping device. It is claimed that, on warm days, the rise in temperature from the reaction makes the drink too hot to handle (Anon, 2002).

Self-cooling cans have also been marketed in Japan for raw sake. The endothermic dissolution of ammonium nitrate and chloride in water is used to cool the product.

## Box 27 - Edible packaging

Although edible packaging might appear to be a modern, niche development, in essence it is the oldest use of packaging - with one type of food being stuffed inside an edible outer coating (e.g. stuffed vine leaves), or with edible coatings being applied to foods (e.g the use of waxes to delay dehydration of citrus fruits). Rice paper (based on rice starch) has long been used as an edible packaging material. Other traditional example include Cornish pasties: in Cornish tin mines, the workers were provided with a savoury first course and sweet dessert at either end of an edible pastry package, part of which was discarded (the thick pastry edge that was held by the consumer). Ice cream cones are another simple form of edible packaging, and sausage casings can also be classified in this way.

Modern developments in edible packaging have focussed on edible films - thin layers or coatings that form an integral part of the food and which are eaten with the food; they can mainly be thought of as edible versions of active or controlled atmosphere packaging. Many of the developments are based on edible films that modify water vapour transfer or which have chemical or microbial preservative properties, but they can also be adapted to encapsulate aroma compounds, pigments, nutrients such as vitamins, or ions to control browning reactions (Debeaufort *et al.*, 1998). The advantage of these films is that the active ingredient will be located in the film, at the surface of the food, which is often where the activity is most required (e.g. for antimicrobial agents or antioxidants). Therefore, actual levels of these additives can be much lower than if they were incorporated throughout the food.

continued...

The primary need of the base film material is that it must capable of forming a cohesive, structural matrix. Zein, a water-soluble protein from maize kernels, has been widely investigated as an edible packaging material; it is an excellent antioxidant for lipids and has good film-forming ability. Collagen, milk proteins, starch and cellulose-based films have also been developed. The choice of material will depend largely on the type of food being packaged and the active function that the film is intended to perform. As well as their inherent properties, the base film will interact differently with the various active components (e.g. antimicrobial agents, antioxidants or water vapour transfer regulators) that are integrated into it.

One piece of research at the University of Bordeaux in France serves as a good example of the interactions that can occur. Attempts were made to improve the moisture barrier properties of an edible film based on hydroxypropylmethyl-cellulose, which is a poor water vapour barrier because of its hydrophilic nature. Hydrophobic compounds were incorporated into the film-forming solution prior to film formation: stearic acid was found to be particularly effective. Nisin was also incorporated into the film to give it the desired antimicrobial properties. However, the presence of stearic acid was found to reduce the antimicrobial effectiveness of nisin (Coma *et al*, 2001).

*Regulatory and safety concerns*

When considering an active packaging development, several regulatory and safety factors have to be considered:

- Legislation regarding materials in contact with food
- Environmental issues
- Labelling to avoid consumer confusion
- The effect of the modified packaging on the microbial flora and safety of the food

Many aspects of these are relevant to all packaging systems. There are, however, some points that are specifically relevant to active packaging systems.

Active packaging substances may migrate into the food or may be removed from it. Migrants may be intended or unintended. Intended migrants include antioxidants, ethanol and antimicrobial preservatives; these need to be specifically permitted in the food in question. Unintended migrants include various metal compounds which achieve their active purpose inside packaging materials but do not need to or should not enter foods. Precautions need to be taken to ensure that accidental contamination is prevented.

Food labelling is necessary to reduce the risk of consumers ingesting the contents of oxygen scavenger sachets or other in-pack active packaging devices. Some active packages may look different from their passive counterparts. Therefore it may be advisable to use appropriate labelling to explain this difference to the consumer even in the absence of regulations.

Finally, it is very important for food manufacturers using certain types of active packaging to consider the effects these will have on the microbial ecology and safety of foods. For example, removing all the oxygen from within packs of high water activity, chilled perishable food products may stimulate the growth of anaerobic pathogenic bacteria such as *Clostridium botulinum*. Specific guidance is available to minimise the microbial safety risks of foods packed under reduced oxygen atmospheres (Betts, 1996). Regarding the use of antimicrobial films, it is important to consider what spectrum of microorganisms will be inhibited. Antimicrobial films that only inhibit spoilage microorganisms without affecting the growth of pathogenic bacteria will raise food safety concerns. Also, preventing the growth of one group of micro-organisms may allow the accelerated growth of others, possibly reducing rather than extending shelf-life.

## 5.3 Intelligent packaging

Intelligent packaging is packaging that in some way senses some properties of the food it encloses or the environment in which it is kept, and which is able to inform the consumer of the state of these properties. Although distinctly different from the concept of active packaging, features can be used to check the effectiveness and integrity of both active and modified atmosphere packaging.

Intelligent packaging devices, which may be an integral component or inherent property of a foodstuff's packaging, can be used to check for tamper evidence and pack integrity, product quality and safety (e.g. through temperature monitoring), and product authenticity, as well as acting as anti-theft devices (e.g. through the use of radio frequency identification (RFID) tagging). There may be considerable overlap in these features. For example, gas sensing dyes can give information on the seal integrity of modified atmosphere packs (i.e. have they been deliberately tampered with or accidentally damaged), and this may provide some indication of product quality and/or safety. Also, some technologies can be applied to address the issues of product authenticity, traceability and anti-theft concurrently (Day, 2000b).

For an intelligent packaging system to be worth installing, it must be inexpensive in relation to the overall value of the product, it must be reliable (both in its technical capabilities and its robustness against routine and excessive wear and tear), and it must be acceptable to the consumer and legislative authorities (i.e. it must be non-toxic, and aesthetically acceptable). It also needs to be compatible with existing distribution and retailing systems (Day, 2000).

*Tamper evidence and pack integrity*

Although deliberate tampering with food packaging, often with the intention of contaminating it in some way (e.g. with poison of some kind), sometimes makes the headlines, it is the casual, almost absent-minded tampering caused by consumers browsing products that is much more of a nuisance to the food industry, and can result in significant financial losses (Day, 2000b).

In the past 10 years or so, this problem has led to the widespread use of many simple devices to indicate if a package has been tampered with in some way. This is usually as simple as indicating whether or not a closure has been opened.

Examples include small shrink-wrapped circles of plastic on a jam jar lids, screw-off plastic or aluminium closures on squash or milk bottles, a foil seal inside the main lid of milk bottles, or vacuum seals on some glass jars - the latter with the notice that if the 'button' in the centre of the lid is not depressed, then jar has been opened. Other simple systems are based on blister, strip and bubble packs, where it is

## Box 28 - Examples of intelligent packaging

Gas-sensing dyes show great promise as means of checking the tamper evidence and seal integrity of modified atmosphere packaging. It is especially critical that this type of packaging is not compromised, as changes in the gas mixture within the package could have serious implications for the quality and safety of the food. A carbon dioxide sensor has been recently introduced that can be placed on the inside of packaging films. At 0% carbon dioxide, the sensor is blue. As the concentration increases, the sensor changes colour to black (10%), brown (20%), green (50%) and yellow (100%).

The 'Fresh-Check' TTI (time-temperature indicator) label contains colourless diacetylene crystals that polymerise to coloured compounds, depending on the temperature and cumulative time for which they are exposed. The time-temperature integration can be related to microbial growth or other temperature-dependent changes in the quality or safety of the product. This relationship needs to be carefully calibrated, as the acceptable storage time and temperature for a chilled product will depend entirely on its formulation. The label consists of a reference ring, resembling a bull's eye, with the colourless crystals inside. When the centre is lighter than the ring, the product is fresh. The end of its shelf-life is reached when the centre is the same colour as the ring. When it becomes darker, it is no longer fit to eat. When using this type of device in retail situations, it is important to ensure that the chemical changes in the indicator actually parallel the changes in the food.

**Reference:**

Day, B.P.F. (2000). Intelligent packaging for foodstuffs. Food Cosmetics and Drug Packaging 23(12): 233-239

subsequently easy to see if the any of contents of the package have been removed (as is widely used in the pharmaceutical industry for packaging tablets).

More sophisticated tamper-evident features rely on chemical reactions, concealed markings and subtle manufacturing techniques. Many techniques have been investigated at laboratory level. Only a limited number have been developed commercially, and these often have quite specific and narrow ranges of usage. Oxygen sensors, for example, which are redox dyes which changes colour depending on oxygen concentration, are primarily used to assure that oxygen has been removed from packaging which contains an oxygen scavenger (i.e. to assure that the scavenger is working). They are very sensitive to oxygen levels above 1% and are not compatible with high carbon dioxide concentrations (Day, 2000b).

*Monitoring quality and safety*

As well as the issues mentioned above, where quality and safety may have been compromised by accidental or deliberate tampering with or damaging the package, there are several scenarios where there may be a need to predict the quality and safety of food within a package. Frozen and chilled foods need to be kept at appropriate low temperatures, and heat-preserved or cooked foods need to have reached certain temperatures for a specified length of time. Some drinks that are best consumed chilled have a label on the packaging that becomes visible at a certain temperature, either indicating that the drink has been adequately chilled, or that it requires refrigeration.

From a safety point of view, there are two main areas where active packaging can be applied. In chilled foods, temperature and time-temperature integrators (devices which indicate if a food has been kept at an elevated temperature, and in the latter case, for how long) can be used to monitor for temperature abuse. At the other end of the spectrum, comparable devices can be used to indicate the adequacy of cooking regimes, most notably in microwave cooking situations, to determine if the required temperature has been reached for long enough. In neither case has the use of these techniques become generally used in the UK.

Other types of device that can indicate the safety or quality of chilled foods include microbial growth indicators, capable of detecting volatile microbial metabolites such as carbon dioxide, hydrogen sulphide, alcohols, sulphur dioxide, acetaldehyde and ammonia. In specific products, characteristic spoilage volatiles could be monitored (e.g. trimethylamine in fresh fish products). Carbon dioxide, being a product of microbial respiration, generally correlates well with microbial growth. However, it is only suitable for products not packed in carbon dioxide-containing modified atmosphere packaging. As with time-temperature indicators, this type of device has not reached mainstream use in retail food packaging.

# 6. FOOD PACKAGING AND THE ENVIRONMENT

Packaging waste management is one of the most significant environmental issues to affect the food and drink industry. As EU legislation changes to increase the percentage of waste packaging that has to be recovered, and with more and more companies coming under the requirements, companies need to be aware of their obligations and what help and information is available. The food industry is subject to the same legislation as other industries with regard to recycling. Coupled with the very special need of the food industry to ensure that the product/packaging combination is both safe and suitable, this imposes quite specific problems on the industry.

The packaging of goods can contribute a significant proportion of the total cost of a product: the food industry, like any other, is always striving to reduce the volume and cost of the packaging it uses wherever possible, within the considerable constraints of ensuring a safe and edible product. This is illustrated by initiatives in the UK, EU and US.

In the UK, packaging waste disposed of by commerce and industry makes up about 3% of the waste stream, and a total (household plus industry) of 7.2 million tonnes of packaging is disposed of to landfill (Incpen, 1999).

There is a general increasing pressure and desire to reduce the amount of waste going to landfill, so there is a need to find alternative methods of treatment and disposal. One way to approach this is to ensure that producers of the commodity that ends up as waste take responsibility for the disposal of that commodity. The idea is that this will minimise the amount of waste that is produced and that, with legislative requirements for this waste to be re-used or recycled, it will influence the design of the commodity so that it becomes more "environmentally friendly", by being easier to recycle. Thus, a type of packaging that was slightly more expensive than alternatives might be used if it could be reused directly, if the alternatives had to be processed for recycling or were only suitable for disposal (e.g. incineration or landfill).

## Box 29 - What is the waste management heirarchy?

The waste management hierarchy is a ranking of the possible treatment and disposal options available for solid waste. The list, in order of preference, aims to promote the use of more environmentally acceptable treatment options in favour of the disposal options.

The hierarchy consists of four main elements which, in order of decreasing favourability, are:

- Waste minimisation - this aims to reduce the quantity of waste generated. It is necessary for some sort of analysis or audit to be completed to highlight inefficiencies in processes where savings could be made.
- Reuse - this involves using materials for their original purpose without major reprocessing. Examples include glass milk bottles, plastic crates, carrier bags and coat hangers.
- Recycling - this involves processing of the waste material to make it into a product, for either a similar use of the material or for use in a completely different product. For example, plastic bottles, once sorted into the various types (e.g. HDPE, LDPE) are chipped and then reformed into plastic bottles again. Composting is also a form of recycling as well as waste-to-energy, where waste is incinerated and used to generate heat and electricity.
- Disposal - the least favourable option - can involve depositing the waste in landfill sites or incineration (without energy recovery and with disposal of the ashes in landfill).

The waste management strategies developed by the UK Government and in Europe promote the higher levels of the hierarchy while trying to reduce dependence on the lower levels. This involves trying to change attitudes - of both businesses and householders - to the reuse and disposal of waste.

From a legislative point of view, in the UK food packaging is defined as all products made of any material that are "used for the containment, protection, handling, delivery and presentation of foods, from raw materials to processed goods, from the producer to the user or the consumer." (Anon, 1997; Anon, 1999); this includes transport or tertiary packaging that is used to "facilitate the handling and transportation of a number of sales units or grouped packaging, to prevent physical handling and transport damage" (e.g. shrink wrapping, cardboard boxes and plastic crates).

The legislation that is driving UK regulations in this area is the European Parliament and Council Directive 94/62/EC of 20 December 1994 on packaging and packaging waste (European Commission, 1994). It aims to harmonise national measures in individual European Community countries in dealing with this type of waste, to limit the impact on the environment and also to ensure that the competition within the internal market is not restricted or distorted. The first priority is to prevent the production of as much packaging waste as possible; this is followed by the desire to increase the recovery and recycling of the waste, thereby reducing the volume for disposal. All packaging that is placed on the market (industrial, commercial, retail, household) comes under this Directive.

The directive set out original aims for packaging recycling, re-use and recovery. Within 5 years of the date when the Directive was implemented into national law:

- between 50 and 65% of packaging waste (by weight) had to be recovered

And of this target:

- between 25 and 45% of packaging waste (by weight) had to be recycled,
- with at least 15% recycled (by weight) for the different types of material that make up packaging (glass, cardboard etc).

Targets are continually being tightened to reduce total waste and increase reuse, recycling and recovery. In the UK the food packaging waste recovery target for 2003 was set at 59%; the material-specific recycling target was set at 19%.

The other main provision was the establishment of "essential requirements" in that the packaging placed on the market has to meet certain specifications. This means that the physical properties and characteristics of the packaging have to allow reuse and/or recycling, whilst ensuring that health and safety issues are taken into account. Another provision of the essential requirements is that the packaging must not contain levels of heavy metals above specified limits. The heavy metals listed are hexavalent chromium, lead, cadmium and mercury and the limits set were a maximum level of 100ppm for the sum of the concentration of each metal compound by June 2001.

The following groups of companies in the EU are defined in the legislation:

- Manufacturers - of the raw material for the packaging
- Converters - who modify the packaging in production/formation of the package
- Packer/fillers - those who put goods into the packaging
- Importers - those who import packaging into the UK
- Sellers - suppliers of packaging to a user or consumer of that package, whether or not filling has taken place

These groups are required to recover packaging waste if the total amount of packaging that they handle is 50 tonnes and their turnover is £2 million. They are required to recover a specific percentage of their packaging waste in order to meet the UK obligations; the limits set in 1999 in the Producer Responsibility Obligations (Packaging Waste) (Amendment No. 2) Regulations are as follows (Anon, 1999), and were still current at the beginning of 2003:

| | |
|---|---|
| Manufacturers | 6% |
| Converters | 9% |
| Packer/fillers | 37% |
| Sellers | 48% |
| Secondary producers | 85% |

Producers are required to be registered with an appropriate agency (the Environment Agency or SEPA, the Scottish Environmental Protection Agency) or with a compliance scheme. Compliance schemes, which are industry-led, take on each of the producer's obligations, thereby making the producer exempt from the obligations, as long as the scheme itself successfully discharges the obligations for recycling and recovery. In effect, this smooths out the problems that might be faced by some smaller companies, who would be unable, in practical terms, to meet the recycling or reclamation requirements of the regulations. Those companies who make up this shortfall, e.g. by providing a greater proportion of recyclable material, would expect to receive financial benefits as a result.

## Box 30 - EPA WasteWise

The U.S. Environmental Protection Agency's WasteWise program is a voluntary program designed to help businesses find practical methods for reducing municipal solid waste through:
• waste prevention
• recyclables collection, and
• purchase or manufacture of recycled products.

The program is designed to help participating companies uncover waste reduction opportunities and set waste reduction goals through:

• a free-phone helpline
• WasteWise representatives, who provide assistance to partner companies; and
• a wide range of waste reduction publications and other services.

EPA provides recognition for individual companies and program successes.

WasteWise partners are asked to conduct waste assessments and then set their own goals to reduce waste, design programs to best implement those goals, and report their progress to the EPA each year.

Established in 1994, WasteWise now has over 1,200 participants: government agencies, universities, hospitals and other organizations committed to cutting costs and conserving natural resources through solid waste reduction.

All organizations within the United States may join the program. Large and small businesses from any industry sector are welcome to participate. Institutions, such as hospitals and universities, and other non-profit-making organizations, as well as state, local, and tribal governments, are eligible to participate in WasteWise.

The WasteWise program targets the reduction of municipal solid waste, such as corrugated containers, office paper, yard trimmings, packaging, and wood pallets. Participants, ranging from small local governments and nonprofit organizations to large, multinational corporations, sign on to the program for a 3-year period.

To help identify measures that can be taken to reduce the amount of waste generated, the EPA suggests that a waste assessment is conducted prior to establishing goals. Once the EPA has approved the goals, companies receive the WasteWise logo for internal and external use, and offers help with drafting press releases and newsletter items to announce a company's commitment to WasteWise.

Sellers of packaging are required to produce information for consumers of goods about return, collection and recovery systems available, their role in the reuse/recycling of the materials and the meaning of markings on packaging. Also, those companies that have a turnover of £5 million or more are required to produce an operational plan to show how they are complying with the regulations, such as evidence of contracts with reprocessors and waste minimisation activities.

Records have to be kept for 4 years. These records must show the amount in tonnes of packaging waste sent to a reprocessor, the breakdown of the type of material sent to the reprocessor and details of the shipments (dates and contact details of reprocessors accepting the waste).

There are an increasing number of logos that are seen on packaging materials. There are no legal requirements to use logos, but if the producer is a member of a recycling scheme (see below) they are required to use the scheme's logo. Typical examples of logos include:

- Logos following variations of three arrows chasing each other in a triangular circle, also known as the Mobius Loop, indicating that the material can be recycled.
- The Mobius Loop, with a % figure in the middle shows that the packaging contains a percentage of recycled material.
- Plastic packaging producers use the American SPI (Society of the Plastics Industry Inc.) coding for showing the type of plastic that the packaging is made from - with a number and the abbreviation of the plastic type detailed within the Mobius Loop.
- The Green Dot scheme is the main recycling scheme at present. The logo is two arrows interlocking with each other, and shows that a fee has been paid for the recovery of the packaging in some European Countries; members of the scheme are required to display this logo on the packaging (Incpen, 2000)

As there is no standardisation for green labelling, the then Department for the Environment, Transport and the Regions (DETR) issued a code of practice for green claims. This document provides some information about what should or what should not be stated, enabling businesses to strengthen their reputation and credibility with consumers, through being able to demonstrate responsibility and meet requirements for some overseas markets (DETR, 2000).

# 7. CONCLUSIONS

Packaging is an essential part of the retail sale of most food and drink products. It serves many inter-related purposes, with the ultimate aim of providing the consumer with safe and palatable products. There are many types of packaging available to the food manufacturer - sometimes the most suitable material for use is fairly straightforward. In other situations, there may be several alternatives, each with their advantages and disadvantages, and the manufacturer needs to make a careful choice of which to use. As well as the obvious constraints of the overall nature of the food or drink, the type of factors that have to be taken into consideration include:

- cost
- attractiveness
- consumer expectation
- compatibility with existing processing equipment
- specific chemical or physical interactions with the product
- product end use (e.g. single portion or repeated use)
- the chance of pack integrity being breached (i.e. the package becoming damaged)
- environmental concerns, such as recyling

In many cases, there will be several equally viable and suitable alternatives, and this is seen with virtually identical competing products appearing in markedly different packaging. Sometimes it may be desirable to use a format that is widely recognised by consumers, in others it may be useful to try a different packaging to highlight a real or perceived difference in the product.

Packaging contributes a significant portion of the overall cost of food production; it is not used unnecessarily. The advent of different plastics and the development of multilayer combinations of plastics, paper and metal now offers the food producer an unparalleled range of choice from which to choose.

# 8. REFERENCES AND FURTHER READING

Those references in bold were of particular use to the author in compiling this overview and the reader may find them of interest if wanting to delve further into the subject of food packaging.

**Air Products (1995). The Freshline guide to modified atmosphere packaging.** Available from Air Products plc, Basingstoke, Hants.

Anon (2002). Self-heat can 'needs improvement'. Food Manufacture, August, 21.

Anon (1999). "The Producer Responsibility Obligations (Packaging Waste) (Amendment No. 2) Regulations 1999". Statutory Instrument 1999 No. 3447.

Anon (1998). The Plastic Materials and Articles in Contact with Food Regulations 1988. Statutory Instrument No. 1376

Anon (1997). The Producer Responsibility Obligations (Packaging Waste) Regulations 1997. Statutory Instrument 1997 No. 648.

Anon. (1996a). Oxygen absorbing packaging materials near market debuts. Packaging Strategies Supplement, January 31 edition, Packaging Strategies Inc., West Chester, PA, USA.

Anon (1996b). The Food Labelling Regulations 1996. Statutory Instrument No. 1499

Anon (1996c). Brewing update. South African Food and Beverage Manufacturing Review 23(9): 19-21,23-24,26

Anon. (1995). Pursuit of freshness creates packaging opportunities. Japanese Packaging News, 12, 14-15.

Anon (1992). Tin in Food Regulations 1992 Statutory Instrument No. 496

Anon (1987). The Materials and Articles in Contact with Food Regulations 1987. Statutory Instrument No. 1523

Arthur Guinness and Co. (1989). Beverage package and a method of packaging a beverage containing gas in solution. US Patent 4,832,968

Bakker, M. (1986). The Wiley Encyclopaedia of Packaging Technology. John Wiley.

**Betts, G.D. (ed.) (1996). Code of practice for the manufacture of vacuum and modified atmosphere packaged chilled foods with particular regard to the risks of botulism. CCFRA Guideline No. 11.**

Braakman, L. (2002). The future of PET. Food Engineering and Ingredients 28 (October): 22-25

**British Glass (1992). Making Glass. Third edition**

British Glass (1996). First class packaging. Video

British Retail Consortium/Institute of Packaging (2002). Technical Standard and Protocol for Companies manufacturing and Supplying Food Packaging Materials for Retailer Branded Products.

**Brody, A. L. and Marsh, K.S. (1997). The Wiley Encyclopaedia of Packaging Technology - 2nd Edition. John Wiley**

Browne, J.J.C. (1996). What widget? Brewer 82(11): 498-503

Brydon, L. (2002). Developments in MAP and active packaging. Proceedings of Minimal Processing Conference, Sardinia.

Burnett, S.-A. and George, R.M. (1993). The effects of chilled cooked meat and carrot piece size on domestic microwave reheating. CCFRA Technical Memorandum No. 688.

Campbell, A.J. (1991). The shelf-stable packaging of thermally processed foods in semi-rigid plastic barrier containers. CCFRA Technical Manual No. 31.

Cocco, D.A. (1986). Poly(vinyl chloride). In: The Wiley Encyclopaedia of Packaging Technology (Ed. M. Bakker). John Wiley

Coma, V., Sebti, I., Pardon, P., Deschamps, A. and Puchavant, F.H. (2001). Antimicrobial edible packaging based on cellulose ethers, fatty acids, and nisin incorporation to inhibit *Listeria innocua* and *Staphylococcus aureus*. Journal of Food Protection 64 (4): 470-475

**Day, B.P.F. (1992). Guidelines for modified atmosphere packaging. CCFRA Technical Manual No. 34.**

Day, B.P.F. (1999). Active packaging of foods. CCFRA New Technologies Bulletin No. 17

Day, B.P.F. (2000a). Chilled food packaging. In: Chilled Foods: A Comprehensive Guide (Eds. C. Dennis and M. Stringer). Publ.: Woodhead Publishing

Day, B.P.F. (2000b). Intelligent packaging for foodstuffs. Food Cosmetics and Drug Packaging 23(12): 233-239

Day, B.P.F. (2001). Fresh prepared produce: GMP for high oxygen MAP and non-sulphite dipping. CCFRA Guideline No. 31.

Debeaufort, F., Quezada-Gallo, J.-A., and Voilley, A. (1998). Edible films and coatings: tomorrow's packagings: a review. Critical Reviews in Food Science and Nutrition 28(4): 299-313

DETR, 2000. "Green Claims Code". Product Code 00EP0437. Available from Defra.

Downing, D.L. (1996). A Complete Course in Canning and Related Processes. Book 2: Microbiology, Packaging, HACCP and Ingredients. 13th edition. CTI Publications.

Du Pont (2003). http://www.dupont.com/industrial-polymers/surlyn

Edwards, M. (1999). Investigation of the sources of tin in canned foods. CCFRA R&D Report 79

Edwards, M. (1999). A survey of tin content of canned pineapple products. CCFRA R&D Report 93

Edwards, M. (1999). A survey of tin content of canned tomatoes and tomato based products. CCFRA R&D Report 96

Environmental Protection Agency (2003). EPA's Wastewise Programme www.epa.gov/wastewise

European Commission, 1994. "European Parliament and Council Directive 94/62/EC of 20 December 1994 on packaging and packaging waste". Official Journal of the European Communities, L 365, 31/12/94, p1-23.

Fath, D. and Soudain, P. (1992). Method for the preservation of fresh vegetables. US Patent No. 5,128,160

Foster, R. (1986). Ethylene-vinyl alcohol copolymers. In: The Wiley Encyclopaedia of Packaging Technology (Ed. M. Bakker). John Wiley

Houston, J.S. (1986). Polystyrene. In: The Wiley Encyclopaedia of Packaging Technology (Ed. M. Bakker). John Wiley

Hurme, E and Ahvenainen, R. (1996). Active and smart packaging of ready-made foods. In: Proceedings of the international symposium on minimal processing and ready made foods. SIK, Göteborg, Sweden, 18-19th April.

Huss, G.J. (1997). Microwaveable packaging and dual-ovenable materials. In: The Wiley Encyclopaedia of Packaging Technology - 2nd Edition (Ed. A.L. Brody and K.S. Marsh). John Wiley

**ILSI (2000). Packaging Materials. 1. Polystyrene for Food Packaging Applications. International Life Sciences Institute.**

**ILSI (2002). Packaging Materials. 2. Polyethylene Terephthalate (PET) for Food Packaging Applications. International Life Sciences Institute.**

Incpen (1999). Pack Facts (minimised). Available from Incpen (Reading, UK) and from www.incpen.org

Incpen (2000). What you need to know about packaging and waste. Information on recovering and recycling used packaging. Available from Incpen or www.incpen.org

Jenkins, W.A. (1997). Regenerated cellulose films. In: The Wiley Encyclopaedia of Packaging - 2nd Edition. (Ed. A.L. Brody and K.S. Marsh). John Wiley.

Labuza, T.P. and Breene, W.M. (1989). Applications of active packaging for improvement of shelf-life and nutritional quality of fresh and extended shelf-life foods. Journal of Food Processing and Preservation, 13, 1-69.

Longworth, R. (1986). Ionomers. In: The Wiley Encyclopaedia of Packaging Technology (Ed. M. Bakker). John Wiley

Lopez, A. A. (1987). A Complete Course in Canning and Related Processes. Book 1 - Basic Information on Canning. 12th Edition. The Canning Trade Inc.

Maraschin, N. J. (1986). Polyethylene, low-density. In: The Wiley Encyclopaedia of Packaging Technology (Ed. M. Bakker). John Wiley

Mihalich, J.M. and Baccaro, L.E. (1986). Polycarbonate. In: The Wiley Encyclopaedia of Packaging Technology (Ed. M. Bakker). John Wiley

Miller, R.C. (1986). Polypropylene. In: The Wiley Encyclopaedia of Packaging Technology (Ed. M. Bakker). John Wiley

Ministry of Agriculture, Fisheries and Food (1997). Survey of lead and tin in canned fruit and vegetables. MAFF Food Surveillance Information Sheet No. 122

Neuman, E.H. (1986). Polyesters, thermoplastic. In: The Wiley Encyclopaedia of Packaging Technology (Ed. M. Bakker). John Wiley

**Page, B. (2001). Metal Packaging - An Introduction. PIRA International Ltd, Leatherhead, Surrey, UK.**

Paine, F.A. and Paine, H.Y. (1983). A Handbook of Food Packaging. Blackie.

Prince, P.E. (1986). Metallizing. In: The Wiley Encyclopaedia of Packaging Technology (Ed. M. Bakker). John Wiley

Rooney, M.L. (1998). Oxygen scavenging plastics for retention of food quality. In: Proceedings of Conference on 'Advances in plastics - materials and processing technology for packaging'. Pira International, Leatherhead, Surrey, UK, 25th February.

Rooney, M.L. (ed.) (1995). Active Food Packaging. Chapman & Hall, London, UK,

Rosato, D.V. (1997). Additives, plastic. In: The Wiley Encyclopaedia of Packaging Technology - 2nd Edition (Ed. A.L. Brody and K.S. Marsh). John Wiley

Rose, D. and Gaze, R.R. (1998). Safe packing of food and drink in glass: guidelines for good manufacturing practice. CCFRA Guideline No. 18

Selke, S. (1997). Understanding Plastics Packaging. Hanser-Gardner.

Smith, M.A. (1986). Polyethylene, high-density. In: The Wiley Encyclopaedia of Packaging Technology (Ed. M. Bakker). John Wiley

**Soroka, W., Emblem, A. and Emblem, H. (1996). Fundamentals of Packaging Technology. Revised UK edition. Institute of Packaging**

Subramaniam, P.J. (1998). Dairy foods, multi-component products, dried foods and beverages. In: Principles and applications of modified atmosphere packaging of foods. B.A. Blakistone (ed.). 2nd edition, Blackie Academic & Professional, London, UK, pp 158-193.

Thorpe, R.H. and Barker, P.M. (1984). Visual can defects. CCFRA Technical Manual No. 10.

Thorpe, R.H. (1994). Guidelines on the prevention of visible can defects. CCFRA Technical Manual No. 37.

Throne, J.L. (1986). Polymer properties. In: The Wiley Encyclopaedia of Packaging Technology (Ed. M. Bakker). John Wiley

Tubridy, M.F. and Sibilia, J.P. (1986). Nylon. In: The Wiley Encyclopaedia of Packaging Technology (Ed. M. Bakker). John Wiley

Turner, T.A. (1998). Canmaking: The Technology of Metal Protection and Decoration. Blackie Academic and Professional

# ABOUT CCFRA

The Campden & Chorleywood Food Research Association (CCFRA) is the largest membership-based food and drink research centre in the world. It provides wide-ranging scientific, technical and information services to companies right across the food production chain - from growers and producers, through processors and manufacturers to retailers and caterers. In addition to its 1500 members (drawn from over 50 different countries), CCFRA serves non-member companies, industrial consortia, UK government departments, levy boards and the European Union.

The services provided range from field trials of crop varieties and evaluation of raw materials through product and process development to consumer and market research. There is significant emphasis on food safety (e.g. through HACCP), hygiene and prevention of contamination, food analysis (chemical, microbiological and sensory), factory and laboratory auditing, training, publishing and information provision. To find out more, visit the CCFRA website at www.campden.co.uk